WHAT TO
PANIC
ATTACKS

BIBLICAL ADVICE FOR OVERCOMING **ANXIETY**

DR. ROBERT BAKSS

Ark House Press
PO Box 1722, Port Orchard, WA 98366 USA
PO Box 1321, Mona Vale NSW 1660 Australia
PO Box 318 334, West Harbour, Auckland 0661 New Zealand
arkhousepress.com

All Scripture quotations are taken from the King James Version.
Special emphasis in verses is added.

First published in 2018 by Ark House Press
Distributed by Lighthouse Publications
A ministry of Lighthouse Baptist Church, Rockhampton
480 Norman Road
Norman Gardens, QLD 4701
Australia
+61 7 4928 6633
church@lighthousebaptist.com.au

For more resources on What to do when Panic Attacks visit: www.robertbakss.com

Cataloguing in Publication Data:
Title: What To Do When Panic Attacks
ISBN: 9780648263906 (pbk.)
Subjects: Mental Health, Healing, Christian Living
Other Authors/Contributors: Bakss, Robert

Cover design: Benjamin Bakss
Layout by initiateagency.com

ENDORSEMENTS

As the unprecedented epidemic of fear and anxiety threaten to destroy our peace of mind, we as a society are left reeling and desperate for answers, practical strategies and hope for freedom. Dr. Robert Bakss provides all three in his new book "What to do when Panic Attacks", in which he discusses the physiological, psychological, emotional and spiritual applications for our lives. Dr. Bakss outlines a comprehensive, wholistic approach to dealing with fear and anxiety, equipping sufferers with tools to overcome this issue in their life. Whether you deal with this dilemma personally or you know someone who does, this book is MUST read for everyone!

Mark and Lesley Henry
ANCHOR Support Group Ministry

As a Psychotherapist, many of the clients I see, suffer with varying degrees of anxiety. Some feel trapped and in bondage to this condition not knowing how to escape. Mental health experts in addressing this epidemic, using various methods of treatment, fail to address this condition from a Biblical perspective. This can leave some clients enslaved to this condition believing there is no way of escape and prone to suffer relapse. Using his extensive Biblical knowledge and insight, Dr. Robert Bakss has skilfully taken God's Word to shed light and provide practical steps that will help professionals and lay people understand the root cause and help sufferers overcome anxiety. This is not just another book on anxiety, it is a practical workbook, a Biblical reference guide and a user manual that can help sufferers overcome this condition successfully.

Barbara Wojtas
Psychotherapist Grad Dip Couns, MACA

TABLE OF CONTENTS

PREFACE

Many years ago I read about an unusual and somewhat humorous incident involving a vacuum cleaner and a parakeet. The name of the bird was Chippy. In one day, he was sucked in, washed up and blown over! The reporter who wrote the article said the problems began when Chippy's owner decided to clean Chippy's cage with a vacuum cleaner. (You can see where this is going!) Chippy's owner removed the attachment from the end of the hose and stuck it in the cage. Just then the phone rang and she turned around to answer it. Barely had she said 'Hello' to the caller when she heard an unusual sound coming from the bird cage. Chippy had been sucked into the vacuum. The bird owner gasped, put down the phone, turned off the vacuum and opened the bag: there was Chippy, still alive but stunned a little. Since the bird was covered with dust and soot, the article went on to say, she grabbed him and raced him into the bathroom and turned on the tap (faucet). She held Chippy under the water for ten minutes to get him clean, nearly drowning him. Then, realizing that Chippy was soaked and shivering and cold 'to the feather', she did what any compassionate bird owner would do; she reached for the hair dryer and blew him dry for ten minutes. Poor Chippy didn't know what hit him! A few days after this drama, the reporter who had initially written about the event contacted Chippy's owner to see how the bird was recovering. 'Well,' she replied, 'Chippy doesn't sing much anymore. He just kind of sits and stares off into space.'

Have you ever felt sucked in, washed up and blown over by life? Do you ever feel like there isn't hope or that you're in a situation leaving you nervous, anxious and just wanting to stare off into space?

Without a doubt I am sure you would agree that life can be pretty tough. Sometimes things hit you all at once and you begin to despair and fret. Then the vicious giant of fear can enter the arena, and before you know it you are facing a battle with anxiety.

In other instances, circumstances or events have not played out the way people had expected and consequently they assume that God is working against them, which only exacerbates the problem of anxiety. As a result of past failures and disappointments, people are filled with doubts, phobias and anxieties and many have become their own worst enemy. They think that life has sucked them in, washed them up and blown them over causing them to be susceptible to panic attacks.

This is why it is vitally important that you understand that there is a God who knows your name and cares about you. He is on your side whether you realise it or not. When the prophet Jeremiah spoke about Ancient Israel's plight and captivity in Babylon, he recorded God's words of encouragement to them. These same words are an encouragement to all who face captivity to anxiety. Listen to the words God told Jeremiah to write: *"For I know the thoughts that I think toward you, saith the LORD, thoughts of peace, and not of evil, to give you an expected end. Then shall ye call upon me, and ye shall go and pray unto me, and I will hearken unto you. And ye shall seek me, and find me, when ye shall search for me with all your heart." (Jeremiah 29:11-13)*. How encouraging to know that God thinks about you and His thoughts are thoughts of peace.

Introduction

YOU'RE UNDER ATTACK!

I'M ATTACKED

When I was a little boy my grandmother, whom we called 'Nana' and my grandfather, whom we called 'Poppy', took my sister Linda, my brother Steven and I to the African Lion Safari drive through park located outside Sydney, Australia. I recall the day well. We were all extremely excited with thoughts of seeing real live lions and lionesses roaming around, whilst we could nervously gaze through the window from the safety of our grandparent's car. Once we arrived at the park we all noticed the signs warning all drivers to ensure the car windows and doors were kept closed. After paying the entry fee and getting the safety briefing, we were on our way and enjoying our safari drive. For our little eyes and eager imaginations it was an amazing sight to see the 'King of the Jungle' in somewhat of a wild setting. We were all thrilled to bits and loved every moment, especially with our grandparents' commentary in elevated tones which increased our excitement. Now in those days there was no air conditioning in cars and the best way to keep cool and get some fresh air was to wind your window down. As we drove through the park my Poppy decided to roll his window down because he was hot. My Nana instantly said, "George wind your window up", to which he replied, "Don't worry Eva, I will if a lion gets too close." My little brother was convinced we were going to be eaten by a lion. However, what we couldn't see was a lion approaching the car from behind. Fortunately a park ranger saw what was happening and noticed the car window down. Using his car megaphone, he screamed at my Poppy through the loud speaker – "Would the gentleman in the green car wind your window up now and drive on." As he was winding the window up it wasn't the sight of the lions near us that shook me, even though it was scary, but what terrified me and caused me to fear was the sound of the roar of a lion. Even though it may have been the lion growling at another lion, it created an intense fear in my heart. I began to agree with my little brother's concerns that we were about to be eaten by lions!

If you have ever heard the guttural roar of a lion, it sounds like the lion is already digesting his last victim. A lion can roar as loud as 114 decibels, about 25 times louder than a lawn mower. It is one of the loudest calls in the animal kingdom and can be heard from up to 8km away. When trying to describe the intensity of a warning cry, the book of Revelation uses the lion's roar as the example, *"And cried with a loud voice, **as when a lion roareth**: and when he had cried, seven thunders uttered their voices." (Revelation 10:3).*

Not all cats roar (which is probably a good thing for those who own housecats), but those that do fascinate us and instil a sense of respect and fear within us when we hear their mysterious and frightening sounds.

When the apostle Peter writes to describe the work of the devil, he does so using the analogy of a roaring lion. In doing so he reminds us that the devil's tactic is to put fear into our heart and mind. He says, *"Be sober, be vigilant; because your adversary* *the devil, **as a roaring lion,** walketh about, seeking whom he may devour:" (1 Peter 5:8).* Peter doesn't refer to the devil as a roaming lion, he refers to him as a roaring lion who roams seeking his next prey.

When you hear a roaring lion and you are under attack, you would think the only reasonable response would be like the Ranger yelling 'Run for your life!' However, contrary to what we might naturally be inclined to do, God instructs us with a different strategy. The Bible says, *"Whom **resist** stedfast in the **faith**, knowing that the same afflictions are accomplished in your brethren that are in the world." (1 Peter 5:9).*

When you are under attack, what is your normal default strategy? Is it flight, freeze or fight? God says 'Fight!'

You are under attack!

The terrorist attacks on the United States that took place by the Islamic terrorist group al-Qaeda on the morning of Tuesday, September 11, 2001, changed the world as we knew it. The September 11 attacks (also referred to as 9/11) killed 2,996 people, injured over 6,000 others and caused at least $10 billion in infrastructure and property damage. Two of the planes were flown into the North and South towers, respectively, of the World Trade Centre complex in New York City, which subsequently caused both 110-story towers to collapse. A third plane crashed into the Pentagon (the headquarters of the United States Department of Defence) in Arlington County, Virginia, leading to a partial collapse of the building's western side. The fourth plane, was initially steered toward Washington, D.C., but crashed into a field near Shanksville, Pennsylvania, after its passengers tried to overcome the Islamic terrorist hijackers. When 9/11 took place, the then President of the United States of America,

President George Bush, was in a Florida school reading a book to elementary kids. Andrew Card, the President's Chief of Staff, entered the room, walked over to the president, and whispered in his ear the infamous words 'America is under Attack.'

In the same way, the apostle Peter is saying to his readers that there will be times when you are under attack. Within this scriptural context, Peter's focus is on cares – otherwise defined as anxieties. Just prior to warning us about the roaring lion, Peter alludes to compounding fears in our life which results in these cares/anxieties. - *"Casting all your care upon him; for he careth for you." (1 Peter 5:7).*

Further on in this book I will discuss these verses in more detail, but suffice it to say that God is using Peter to help us understand the devil causes attacks on your faith to produce fear. This is why the Bible connects the purpose of the lion's roar to fear, *"The **fear** of a king is **as the roaring of a lion**: whoso provoketh him to anger sinneth against his own soul." (Proverbs 20:2).* Also, *"The **lion hath roared**, who will not **fear**? the Lord GOD hath spoken, who can but prophesy?" (Amos 3:8).*

The fear generated in our hearts is designed to produce care/anxiety in order to create a flight response, then panic attacks you.

When preying on animals, a lion will often roar. The terrifying sound is calculated to scare the prey and subsequently cause them to flee from their hiding place or run and isolate themselves from their herd as they try to escape the paws and jaws of the lion. When the animal runs, it places itself out in the open and becomes an easier catch for the lion. – *"Will a lion roar in the forest, when he hath no prey? will a young lion cry out of his den, if he have taken nothing?" (Amos 3:4).*

Satan will use whatever means possible to put fear into us and get us to run from our place of safety in God. When fear begins to take control of our heart and mind, and forms the reason behind our decisions and choices, we are bound to end up in trouble.

When panic attacks – What are you to do?

Are you plagued by fears, phobias, or panic attacks? Do you toss and turn at night with a knot in your stomach, worrying about your job, your family, your work, your health, or your relationships? Do you suffer from crippling shyness, obsessive doubts, or thoughts and feelings of insecurity? If you answered, "Yes" to any of those questions, then you more than likely have suffered with anxiety and possibly panic attacks. This area of mental health impacts many people.

The psychiatric medical dictionaries define a panic attack as an episode of acute, intense anxiety, characterized by thoughts of impending doom with symptoms such as pounding or racing heart, sweating, trembling or shaking, feelings of choking or smothering, chest pain, nausea, dizziness, feelings of unreality, and chills or hot flashes. Attacks usually occur suddenly, last from a few seconds to an hour or longer, and vary in frequency from several times a day to once a month.[1] A panic attack is also often referred to as an anxiety attack because the immediate cause of the attack is anxiety which may be caused by a range of factors and issues.

Anxiety and panic attacks are the unwelcome visitors many of us can do without. The dread of having an attack is an awful feeling and often compounds the problem. At times coming out of seemingly nowhere, panic attacks transform the ordinary world of everyday life into a nightmare of anxiety and suffering.

My wife, Jenny, who has suffered with bipolar disorder for the last twenty-four years, has also suffered with panic attacks a few times throughout the stages of her mental illness. As her husband I have witnessed the effects of panic attacks, and have helped her through several episodes during our journey together. We have

---

1 https://medical-dictionary.thefreedictionary.com/panic+attack

faced the roar of the lion and in spite of every inclination to run in fear, we have followed Biblical principles to resist the devil and battle the anxiety.

One thing to remember is this –
You are not alone.

Dr. Archibald Hart, Christian psychologist and expert on stress and anxiety, says in his book, "The Anxiety Cure," that *"many hard-working, driven people (like you and me) don't realize just how close [we] walk to the precipice of anxiety until one day, out of the blue, a panic attack strikes . . . We don't realize how close we are to the edge of anxiety until we lose our footing and tumble . . . into the dark abyss of panic."*[2]

Well-known pastor and author, Louie Giglio, has recently spoken out about his struggle with depression and anxiety. He described his mental health battle beginning early one morning in autumn of 2008. Giglio said that he went to bed one night like any other, but that he woke up at 2 a.m. with a horrendous and terrifying panic feeling that completely overtook and consumed him. He said in an interview, *"I thought I was dying right there on the spot. I think in the old days, we called it a nervous breakdown, but we don't use those terms anymore. I think it's too pejorative for our politically correct world to say that, so now we say people have a panic disorder or an anxiety attack. I definitely had both of those things, but it was worse than that - it was more than that. The symptoms were crazy, and the result was that I was incapacitated— out of work, didn't leave the house a lot of days, going from doctor to doctor, living under a cloud of doom and dread and worry ... just*

2 https://hope1032.com.au/stories/faith/2017/pressing-panic-button/

stagnant. What followed was a very slippery and quick slope into a pit, which you can label anxiety, depression, fear, worry – all of it stemming out of depression." Giglio concluded, *"And I spent about four months of my life in a tunnel of darkness. I thought I was going insane."*

The preacher, who is also known for founding the Passion Conferences (gatherings that include tens of thousands of Christian young adults) said that he went to 15 doctors to get checked out for everything imaginable. Over time, Giglio eventually regained his sanity and although he says he has now improved, it remains a *"thorn"* which is always at risk of reappearing. *"I understand that at any day now, if I don't listen to God, I could end up in that place again,"* he said. *"It's God's story of grace. It's not my story of strength."* He continues and gives some great hope and encouragement to others when he said, *"I thought I was off the rails for good, but as God does, He meets us in the dark, and He leads us into the light. He did that for me — it wasn't a simple or easy process, but God did bring me back, all the way back. I've seen Him do that, time and time again, in other people's lives as well."*[3]

We live in the age of anxiety and the roaring lion is constantly using media, news, calamities, disputes and troubles as his fear tactics designed to make us anxious. So, as we begin our journey into the sources of anxiety and the solutions to this debilitating condition, may the God of peace speak peace to your hearts and minds through His Word and the principles within this book.

---

3 http://www.homecomingmagazine.com/article/the-comeback-kid-louie-giglio/

Part 1

THE SOURCES OF ANXIETY

Chapter 1

WHAT IS ANXIETY?

I'M ANXIOUS

Fightings within, and Fears without[4]

Surpassing even depression, anxiety is the most common form of mental health condition in Australia. On average, one in four people (one in three women and one in five men) will experience anxiety at some stage in their life. It's estimated that approximately 10 percent of teenagers suffer from an anxiety disorder of some kind.[5]

Approximately 5 percent of the population will experience full blown panic attacks at some time or another. The chances are fairly high that either you or a loved one has had a history of anxiety. In a twelve-month period, over two million Australians experience anxiety. In the United States the figure is more like forty million people. You can't ignore this problem. Anxiety is BIG!

Anxiety disorders can take a number of forms and will affect

---

4 This phrase is a line from the Hymn, "Just as I am" by Charlotte Elliot, which describes her battle with mental and emotional pain - https://www.challies.com/articles/hymn-stories-just-as-i-am/
5 https://www.beyondblue.org.au/the-facts

everyone differently. However, common to all disorders is anxiety so distressing it can interfere with a person's ability to carry out, or take pleasure in day-to-day life. Severe anxiety is a feature of a group of mental health disorders including:

- **Generalised anxiety disorder** - persistent, excessive or unrealistic worries about everyday issues or events.
- **Panic disorder** – sudden onset of panic attacks.
- **Social anxiety disorder** - intense excessive worry about social situations.
- **Specific phobias** - an intense, irrational fear of everyday objects and situations.
- **Obsessive compulsive disorder (OCD)** - compulsions and obsessions which a person can't seem to control.
- **Post-traumatic stress disorder (PTSD)** - recurrent and intrusive memories of a trauma, feelings of emotional numbing and detachment, and increases in emotional arousal, such as irritability and disturbed sleep, resulting from a previous traumatic event.[6]

With 25 percent of the adult population having a diagnosable mental disorder called anxiety, only about one-third of them are getting any treatment. The other two-thirds are trying to manage their anxiety by themselves. All the while anxiety is trying to bury them.

What we do know is that anxiety is an increasing problem affecting more and more people every year. If you do a Google search on the word "anxiety" you will quickly see how many sites are listed. At the time of writing this book the number was 79 million!

---

6 https://www.blackdoginstitute.org.au/clinical-resources/anxiety/what-is-anxiety

An interesting study carried out in the United States showed that anxiety in children and college students has increased substantially since the 1950s. In fact, according to Robert Leahy, director of American Institute of Cognitive Therapy, the average high school student today has the same level of anxiety as the average psychiatric patient in the early 1950s.7 Anxiety has been increasing and we are getting more anxious every decade.

How do you define anxiety?

Anxiety is the present emotion of fear and inner turmoil produced by the uncertainty of the future. We actually feel anxiety in our bodies.[8]

Everyone feels anxious from time to time. Feeling anxious in certain situations can help us avoid danger, triggering our *'fight or flight'* response. However when we become overly worried and fearful about a threat or bad things that may or may not happen, our persistent worry and fear become out of proportion to the reality of the threat. This ends up leading a person to suffer from anxiety.

Anxiety is more than just feeling stressed or worried. It is the painful uneasiness of the mind that feeds on impending fears. In its mildest form we simply churn. In its most severe form we panic.

When the physical symptoms of stress and worry don't subside, and they become an ongoing issue in our lives, this is when anxiety can kick in. However, sometimes without notice people can suffer from an anxiety attack without discerning any particular reason, stress or cause at the time.

---

7 https://www.psychologytoday.com/blog/anxiety-files/200804/how-big-problem-is-anxiety
8 https://medical-dictionary.thefreedictionary.com/anxiety

Stressing out over a meal

In the Bible, Jesus corrected a woman named Martha for allowing her worries to consume her and affect her home, work and ultimately her peace. Martha was stressing about a catering event, and lack of help caused her to become anxious. Imagine if the main thing ever recorded about you in history was that the day Jesus came to your house for dinner you had a bad attitude, and when you complained to Jesus, he told you off! Then we use your name for generations to come as an illustration of why we should not act like that. Ouch!

This account is found in Luke 10:38-42. Jesus was visiting the house of his good friends Lazarus and his sisters Martha and Mary. He visited this house on several occasions and in fact the apostle John records that Jesus loved Lazarus and his two sisters Mary and Martha: *"Now Jesus loved Martha, and her sister, and Lazarus."* *(John 11:5).* Whenever Jesus wanted to come aside and have a break, He knew He could go to Bethany and Martha would have something ready for him. Martha had the cupboard stocked and ready for Jesus. She would serve Him his favourite dish (maybe fish and chips). I am sure Jesus had his favourite chair, pillow, and place to sit. There were things that kept bringing Him back there that ministered to His humanity and refreshed Him as a person.

On the occasion of this visit the Lord and his weary and hungry disciples just drop in and no doubt their friends were delighted to see Jesus. Martha immediately starts to get some food ready and the Gospel writer Luke moves quickly to describe her actions. *"Now it came to pass, as they went, that he entered into a certain village: and a certain woman named Martha received him into her house. And she had a sister called Mary, which also sat at Jesus' feet, and heard his word. But Martha was cumbered about much serving, and came to him, and said, Lord, dost thou not care that my sister hath left me to serve alone? bid her therefore that she help me." (Luke 10:38-40).*

We can visualise her rushing around, clanging pots and then becoming anxious when she realised the huge job on her hands – *"But Martha was **cumbered** about **much serving**."* To be cumbered means to be "full, loaded up, distracted or troubled". She felt overwhelmed.

Lack of hospitality in that culture was a sign of rudeness and maybe these expectations played on her mind. Her sister Mary, on the other hand, realising the rarity of the visit, sits and listens to the Lord speak to his disciples and Lazarus.

In the text we see the tension that Martha's service created. In her busyness Martha gets snippety at her sister who, in her eyes, was just sitting down listening to Jesus teach. What we witness in this encounter is a worrier, a woman full of care. The cares of the world have choked the happiness and life out of her. Martha's out-of-balance concerns over the meal preparations prevented her from focusing on the Lord.

Blaming Jesus for your anxiety

Whatever Martha has already done to get Mary's attention, she is totally exasperated now and speaks directly to Jesus. Her level of anxiety causes her to even accuse Jesus of not caring about her plight, *"**Lord, dost thou not care** that my sister hath left me to serve alone?"* The pressure had got to her and she snapped. When your anxiety reaches a certain point it is not uncommon to exhibit the emotion of anger and lash out at others. You get angry at yourself, or angry with anyone else who you think might have made a difference. Martha is so angry she doesn't even call her sister by name as she suggests the solution to Jesus. The harder Martha worked the more worked up she became and in doing so became full of care or anxiety.

Her accusation of Jesus not caring was quite ironic considering it was this very issue of her own care that was the reason she was feeling this way. This prompted Jesus to reply to her, *"Martha, Martha, thou art **careful** and **troubled** about many things: But one thing is needful: and Mary hath chosen that good part, which shall not be taken away from her." (Luke 10:41-42).*

Gentle Jesus pinpointed Martha's trouble with precise accuracy as He peered into her soul. She had allowed the anxiety of the moment to cloud her attitude and steal her joy. I imagine Martha's facial expressions and her body language betrayed her internal stress. While the pots were boiling on the stove she was boiling on the inside.

Like Martha, we can get so distracted by all the seemingly necessary things that we miss the point. The more we worry, the more it slows us down. Have you ever felt so worried you felt like you were living in slow motion?

Anxiety is like a computer virus that we carry around. Just as the computer virus slows down the operating functions on the computer, so too anxiety subtly slows us down and quietly keeps us from operating at full speed. It runs in the background of our lives and has the potential to shut down our lives. Anxiety ultimately hurts us and helps no one.

Author, Jodi Picoult, described anxieties as useless and helpless when she said, "Anxiety's like a rocking chair. It gives you something to do, but it doesn't get you very far."[9]

On a positive note, the next time we read of Martha cooking up a feast she is no longer anxious and overwhelmed. She had learnt

---

9 www.anxiety.org/jodi-picoult-anxiety-is-like-a-rocking-chair-inspirational-quotes

to bring her cares to Jesus rather than accuse Him of not caring. Martha got victory over her anxiety. *"Then Jesus six days before the passover came to Bethany, where Lazarus was which had been dead, whom he raised from the dead. There they made him a supper; and **Martha served**: but Lazarus was one of them that sat at the table with him." (John 12:1-2).*

What do people experience if they have an anxiety disorder?

A person with an anxiety disorder may feel distressed a lot of the time, even if there seems to be no obvious reason. An episode can be so severe it is debilitating. Anxiety hits everyone differently but there are common threads, signs and symptoms.

A person may be thinking:
- 'Everything's going to go wrong'
- 'I might die'
- 'I can't handle the way I feel'
- 'I can't focus on anything but my worries'
- 'I don't want to go out today'
- 'I can't calm myself down'.

A person might be feeling:
- Very worried or afraid most of the time
- Tense and on edge
- Nervous or scared
- Panicky
- Irritable, agitated
- Worried you're going crazy

- Detached from your body
- Feeling like you may vomit.

A person may also be experiencing:
- Sleep problems (can't get to sleep, wake often)
- Pounding heart
- Sweating
- 'Pins and needles'
- Tummy aches, churning stomach
- Light-headedness, dizziness
- Twitches, trembling
- Problems concentrating
- Excessive thirst.[10]

Some of these symptoms can also be signs and symptoms of other medical conditions, so it's always best to see a doctor who can check them properly. Sometimes, when we're anxious, we can feel symptoms that we might think are other health problems. Severe anxiety can result in chest pain, a racing heartbeat, dizziness and even rashes. Sometimes anxious people think they're having a heart attack but are not, it can simply be anxiety. You should always see a doctor regardless, so he or she can make a thorough check of your symptoms and rule out any other medical condition.

Where does anxiety come from?

Anxiety disorders are thought to be caused by a combination of a complex set of risk factors that may trigger anxiety or make it worse, including:
- Genetic vulnerability to develop an anxiety disorder

10 www.sane.org/mental-health-and-illness/facts-and-guides/anxiety-disorder

- Personality traits
- Brain chemistry
- Trauma
- Responses to stressful life events and stress build up
- Stress due to an illness
- Other mental health disorders, such as depression
- Drugs or alcohol.[11]

I would add to this list an area that the medical profession often overlook - spiritual warfare. The apostle Paul spoke of the battles a Christian will face. He wrote, *"Put on the whole armour of God, that ye may be able to stand against the wiles of the devil. For we wrestle not against flesh and blood, but against principalities, against powers, against the rulers of the darkness of this world, against spiritual wickedness in high places." (Ephesians 6:11-12).*

When seeking to manage, reduce or even eliminate the symptoms associated with anxiety disorders there are a few mainstay practices in the medical profession. At times a doctor may prescribe medication to help a person, however the most effective treatment for most people affected by anxiety disorders is psychological therapy. It is with this in mind and coupled with Biblical principles that I believe the best treatment to aid with anxiety is the Word of God and the Holy Spirit providing cognitive therapy in the heart and mind of the sufferer.

We will now discuss the Biblical principles surrounding the sources of anxiety and the solutions that God offers through His Word.

---

11 https://www.mayoclinic.org/diseases-conditions/anxiety/symptoms-causes/syc-20350961

Chapter 2

THE WIND AND WAVES WITHIN

I'M AFRAID

Fear is the ultimate source of Anxiety

Each one of us can either be fuelled by unhealthy fear or fuelled by faith. When we face trying circumstances and pressures of life, we don't want to be people fuelled by fear. Rather, we must strive to be people of faith who face the trials and troubles of life with a firm belief in God and adherence to His Word. Otherwise fear can fuel the journey of life and bring about an anxious state of mind and heart.

In my own life I have seen God do some amazing things which has fuelled my faith in Him. It's my desire that this book will help people move from fear to faith in God through His Word.

When it comes to the battle with anxiety and facing the lion's roar two things are at stake – your sanity and the glory of God. Nothing steals God's glory more than worrying believers who are driven through life by fear.

Fear is an emotion caused by the belief of a looming potential danger or loss. Anxiety is the by-product of our ability to remember the past and project into the future. It's our ability to remember what happened the last two times we had a family reunion and then project that experience into the future and look forward with excitement to or dread the next family reunion depending on your past experiences. Fear is a lack of confidence in self or others to control the situation. Anxiety comes when you think you can't pull it off and you are not in control. On the contrary, faith is confidence in God to control the situation.

I read about a young truck driver in the United States of America whose route takes him across the Chesapeake Bay Bridge in Maryland every day. The thought entered his mind that he just might feel compelled to stop the truck, climb out, and leap from the bridge to his death. There was no rational reason to hold such a belief, but that very fear took complete hold of him. He finally asked his wife to handcuff him to the steering wheel so he could be fully assured that his deepest fear wouldn't come true. That's exactly what fear does when we allow it to have power over us; it shackles our hands and keeps us from doing the routine things in life, working, playing, living, and serving God. We give in to the slavery of terror.

Fear has been described as a small trickle of doubt that flows through the mind until it wears such a great channel that all your thoughts drain into it. Tiny fears, almost unperceived, can build up day by day until we find ourselves paralysed and unable to function and living in a constant state of anxiety. There is something very predictable about fear: it distorts our view and skews our perspective.

The primary purpose of the devil's roaring like a lion is to produce fear in your life. Using any means necessary, Satan and his demons have a seemingly endless supply of tools they use to pluck up the seeds of the implanted Word of God in your heart.

Whatever tool he uses, whether it be: lies, doubts, accusations and slander in your mind, sickness, torments, hindrances or division, and however he uses them, they all lead to fearfulness. When fear takes control and creates anxiety it will not be long before panic attacks you.

I heard, I was afraid so I hid

If you cast your mind back to the Genesis account of the fall of man in the Garden of Eden, you will notice the response of Adam after he sinned. The voice of God called out to him, and he and his wife, Eve, had become hopelessly lost in lies. Fear was fuelling their lives and competing for their attention and dominating their decisions. The Bible records the event as follows; *"And the LORD God called unto Adam, and said unto him, Where art thou? And he said, **I heard** thy voice in the garden, and **I was afraid**, because I was naked; and **I hid myself.**" (Genesis 3:9-10).*

This passage of Scripture gives us a vital and important insight in the operation of fear. Once the devil's roar has frightened us and convinced us of his lie, that God is against us and has let us down, fear seizes hold of our heart and drives us into hiding and isolation, just as it did with Adam: "I heard you, I was afraid of you so I hid from you God." The last person we want to face is God and yet He is the only one who can truly help. This is the dangerous strategy of the roaring lion, Satan.

Many of us may recall childhood moments of terror that etch vivid events into our memory banks. It is amazing how years later a similar event can trigger us to replay the terrorising memories and the fear of the past is immediately transported to become the fear of the present. Even if the childhood fears were irrational fears, they still torment us. We then start to play out the endless 'what-if' scenarios in our minds increasing the fear and anxieties. We start to question ourselves and the answers we get back cause us to retreat into hiding.

- What if I look like an idiot if I try this new venture and it doesn't work? *I then let fear squash my dream.*
- What if they think I'm stupid because I ask a question that is basic knowledge to everyone else? *I let fear silence me and don't ask the question.*
- What if they interpret my asking a question as a sign of weakness or incompetence and lose respect for me? *Again, fear squashes my desire to learn, and remain ignorant.*
- What if they take advantage of me? *Fear stops me doing a good deed and others miss out.*
- What if they don't even want my help and end up rejecting me? How will I handle that?
- What if I give generously and then don't have enough to meet my own needs?
- What if I go out of my way and nobody appreciates it?
- What if I tell him how I feel, trying to get the relationship back to a place that honours God, and he turns it on me and it's worse than before?
- What if they don't call? What if they do?
- What if I don't get offered the job? What if I do?
- What if the alarm doesn't go off? What if it goes off and I don't hear it?
- What if I forgot something? What if I remember?
- What if I marry her and she's not the one? What if I marry her and she is the one but I don't like being married?

The world of what-ifs is a black hole, and it will suck your joy, peace, and hope into its vortex if you venture near its vicinity. The what-if's are endless causes that create fear and anxiety.

My wife, Jenny, says she is more vulnerable to hurtful fears through intrusive and unwanted thoughts that can easily trigger anxiety. When the low hits her and depression overwhelms her mind, it is then that fears start to dominate her thinking and if she allows it to stay – panic attacks.

Love versus Fear

We fear terrorist attacks and doctor's reports that might reveal a cancer. We fear opening e-mails that might contain bad news about our business or from our boss or a hurtful remark from a sibling.

These fears don't just go away. In fact, if left alone, they tend to compound, spread, and destroy. They build, and before we know it they form levels of anxiety and terror that will annihilate our awareness of the love of God. The apostle John reminds us that knowing you are loved of God has power to stop fear from entering your life. It's like God's love stands at the door of your heart like a bouncer at a posh restaurant and prohibits fear from entering. - *"There is no fear in love; but **perfect love casteth out fear**: because **fear hath torment**. He that feareth is not made perfect in love." (1 John 4:18).* You have to kick fear out of your heart and mind or it will torment you and keep you trapped in anxiety.

To overcome the paralysis of fear you must take a step of faith and decide to take your stand in the love of God in the battle against fear. Fear has no choice but to relocate when God's love grabs it by the collar and says, 'You're not welcome here.'

We can either hide like Adam when we are afraid and believe the lies of the devil that God's love is conditional and He has given up on us. Or we can respond to the voice of fear and fight back standing in the confidence that God's love is unconditional and everlasting. *"The LORD hath appeared of old unto me, saying, Yea, I have loved thee with an everlasting love: therefore with lovingkindness have I drawn thee." (Jeremiah 31:3).*

A panic attack at sea

One of the great stories in the Gospel accounts of the life of Jesus is when He and his disciples were caught in a storm on the Sea of Galilee, and his disciples allowed the *'what-if's'* to play out various scenarios in their minds. Eventually they vocalised their panic attack and accused Jesus of not caring.

Before we look at the incident, let's first go back in the Gospel of Mark and listen to what Jesus had been teaching on the day of the storm. Jesus had been teaching His famous parable concerning the sower and the seed. The sower represented Jesus, the seed was the Word of God and the four soil types each represented the various receptive natures of the heart of the listeners. One of the soil types was thorny ground which grew up and choked out the fruitfulness of the plant. Jesus gave the interpretation of this parable and said *"And these are they which are sown among thorns; such as hear the word, And the **cares** of this world, and the deceitfulness of riches, and the lusts of other things entering in, choke the word, and it becometh unfruitful." (Mark 4:18-19).*

It is interesting to note that Jesus had just preached on the *"cares of the world"*, fear being like a thorn that chokes out the Word of God. He then got in a ship and sowed the seed of faith into the soil of the disciple's hearts. Their response revealed the type of heart they had. Jesus gave them His Word that they would get to the other side of the sea. *"And the same day, when the even* was come, he saith unto them, Let us pass over unto the other side." (Mark 4:35).

They began their journey and a storm broke out – "And when they had sent away the multitude, they took him even as he was in the ship. And there were also with him other little ships. And there arose a great storm of wind, and the waves beat into the ship, so that it was now full." (Mark 4:36-37). I want you to notice there was wind and waves creating unrest and turmoil and eventually fear.

But where was Jesus in this moment of terror? He was full of peace and sleeping whilst the disciples were being choked by cares. "And he was in the hinder part of the ship, asleep on a pillow: and they awake him, and say unto him, Master, carest thou not that we perish?" (Mark 4:38). Jesus was so peaceful that the Bible even described his restful state of being "asleep on a pillow." No doubt the wind and waves caused water to splash onto Jesus, yet He was sound asleep and full of peace.

On the other hand the disciples were under attack. Fear created care/anxiety and panic set in and the worst case scenario was being played out in the minds of the disciples. They awoke the Saviour and accused him saying, in effect, "Don't you CARE? We are full of CARE right now and you're sleeping. We are having a panic attack. Jesus, aren't you anxious? Don't you care?"

Panic attacks are the result of increased care or anxiety. We get anxious about an uncertainty, doubt, abstract threat and worry. Fear undealt with will produce anxiety with a perceived imminent threat. With that fear, adrenaline is released and panic attacks.

Panic attacks are the result of an overstimulated stress response from some ongoing fear - fear of failure, fear of losing control, fear of not measuring up, and so forth. Fear keeps the stress hormones flowing, which in turn generate certain discomforting physical sensations. They occur when anxiety triggers hyperventilation (rapid and shallow breathing), which results in too little carbon dioxide in the lungs. This changes the pH level of the plasma and leads to the tingly, light-headed, unreal, panicky feelings. We don't know what physical sensations the disciples were having but we do know they hit the panic button.

When anxiety controlled by fear strikes your life it affects the mind. But God doesn't desire this and states in the Bible; *"For God hath not given us the spirit of fear; but of power, and of love, and of a sound mind."* (2 Timothy 1:7).

Peace be still

Jesus then taught the disciples a visual lesson on how to calm the wind and waves within. With three words Jesus calmed the wind and waves – *"And he arose, and rebuked the wind, and said unto the sea, **Peace, be still**. And the wind ceased, and there was a great calm."* (Mark 4:39). Jesus spoke out what was within Him – Peace. He then dealt with the issue at hand. He told them their lives were being fuelled by fear instead of faith, *"And he said unto them, Why are ye so **fearful**? how is it that ye have **no faith**?"* (Mark 4:40). Jesus had told them they were going to the other side. He had given them His Word and they had not placed faith in the Word of God and His promise.

We can produce our own wind and waves within our hearts and minds through various means.

Firstly with our own words. Our world is created by our words, the things we say within. This is often referred to as self-talk. We may not even audibly utter the words but we think them and say them in our minds, like "I'm never going to be able to…", "I know it won't work out", "They are right, I am useless and can't…" These types of negative, self-fulfilling prophecies of doom are creating winds and waves of unrest and turmoil within. Fears and especially irrational fears will produce winds and waves of care/anxiety. These are the *what if* and the *if only* thoughts that plague our minds. They are the recurring thoughts of doubt and uncertainties. We say things like:

- "I just know my mind will go blank when I give my presentation at work, and everyone will think I'm an idiot." Fear leads to a panic attack!
- "I just know I'll freeze up and blow it when I take my test."
- "Everyone at this party can see how nervous I am."
- "Flying is so dangerous. I think this plane is going to crash"
- "I shouldn't be so anxious and insecure. Other people don't feel this way."
- "I feel like I'm on the verge of cracking up."
- "What's wrong with me? I'm such a loser."
- "Why can't I get anything done? My life seems like one long procrastination."

Secondly, we create winds and waves within by the way we approach things. Our own lack of organisation or planning may very well be the catalyst to bring about a stressful moment that triggers a sense of fear and anxiety. For example, it was not the class that was stressful but your procrastination in accomplishing the tasks required in the class that made it stressful. Your approach to life may be the cause of winds and waves within.

Thirdly, through listening to wrong voices. Listening to stressful news can create winds and waves within. Do you really need to be worried about every bit of news in countries you can't even pronounce? If I listen to depressive news and information constantly it can create waves of worry and produce care and anxiety. I am literally making my own waves by the choices I make in feeding my mind and heart. In our social media saturated world, there is way too much intake and we are filling up every spare space with these voices. We are tuning into the frequencies broadcasting fear and then praying for the peace of God but He has nowhere to put it. We have to make a place for peace.

Where is your focus?

The truth is fear and faith are both energised by focus, and when panic attacks, we must put our focus on God and His Word by faith. Using His Word, Jesus spoke peace to the wind and the waves without. Likewise, we are able to speak peace to the wind and waves within our soul by applying His Word to our fears.

The lesson for us is in the storms of life to fuel our faith, we must expel the fears knowing that God loves us and has our best interest at heart. We must trust in his Word and place our faith in Him and keep our eyes off the storm. We literally counteract fear with faith in the promises of God.

In times of winds and waves within Jenny's life, her focus would be directed to faith in the Word of God and specific promises. In particular two verses of scripture have proven to be a great comfort to calm the storms within. The first passage is *"What time I am afraid, I will trust in thee. In God I will praise his word, in God I have put my trust; I will not fear what flesh can do unto me." (Psalm 56:3-4).* The other passage is *"Fear ye not, neither be afraid: have not I told thee from that time, and have declared it? ye are even my witnesses. Is there a God beside me? yea, there is no God; I know not any." (Isaiah 44:8).*

Watch what happens within when faith is wavering in our lives.

James says *"But let him ask in faith, nothing wavering. For he that wavereth is like a **wave** of the sea driven with the **wind** and tossed. For let not that man think that he shall receive any thing of the Lord. A double minded man is unstable in all his ways. (James 1:6-8).*

The real waves are not on the outside but on the inside. I need to speak peace to the winds and the waves within by holding on to the promises of God. Jesus is using the outside winds and waves as the illustration for His disciples. He is saying to them and to us, "What I just did to the wind and the waves, you need to do to what's inside of you. Wake up your faith and speak peace to the winds and the waves within."

The narrative concluded with another statement on fear but this time the fear was directed toward God. This is a healthy fear. *"And they feared exceedingly, and said one to another, What manner of man is this, that even the wind and the sea obey him?" (Mark 4:41).* As the context reveals, their terror was no longer connected to what they were going through. What made them fear exceedingly was to witness the power of His Word. They saw that His Word could calm the wind and the waves. He is the creator of the winds and waves and therefore they have to obey Him.

What happened to the disciples through this event was a shift in their hearts. It is the same shift that can take place in each of our hearts. At the beginning of the storm the disciples were fearful and panicking because of the wind and waves without. However, after they saw what Jesus did, their fear of the storm was shifted to their fear of God. Their fear of someone overwhelmed their fear of something. They knew then they didn't need to fear the wind and the waves when they had the Master of the sea in their ship. His words within are louder than the wind and the waves within.

Chapter 3

WATER WALKERS

I'M APPREHENSIVE

Fear breeds Doubt as a source of Anxiety

Storm-chasing is the pursuit of any severe weather condition, regardless of motive, which can be curiosity, adventure, scientific investigation, or for news or media coverage. Avid, dedicated storm chasers are always looking for the perfect storm. No-one could create a perfect storm like Jesus.

When we talk of storms in life we refer to a time of trouble or difficulty such as a family dilemma, a financial crisis or crunch time, perhaps a sickness that is unexpected or lingers on. For some the storm may come in the form of temptations that continue to batter us like the fierce waves smashing the shoreline during a cyclone. You are just battling away and looking for a way out. But some are just looking for answers. For many people the storm of fear and anxiety seems like a storm that never ends.

In the last chapter I referred to a storm incident on the Sea of Galilee that produced a panic attack in the lives of the disciples. Upon waking Jesus from His sleep, He was able to calm the storm without on the sea and within the disciples.

In 2016 I visited Israel and took the customary tourist cruise on the Sea of Galilee. It was a fascinating and surreal experience to think I was sailing on the very waters that Jesus walked upon! Whilst I was there the sea was very calm and I inquired whether the waters of the great inland lake ever became difficult to sail on due to stormy weather. The guide informed me that in certain conditions the winds can whip across the sea creating huge waves and in fact the place was known for its sudden storms.

On the Sea of Galilee, it may be said that storms will come suddenly, and unexpectedly, which illustrates for Christians that they can expect storms to erupt suddenly as well for them.

Contrary winds create perfect storms

Another perfect storm incident with Jesus and His disciples on the Sea of Galilee is recorded in Mark Chapter 6 as follows; *"And straightway he constrained his disciples to get into the ship, and to go to the other side before unto Bethsaida, while he sent away the people. And when he had sent them away, he departed into a mountain to pray. And when even was come, the ship was in the midst of the sea, and he alone on the land. And he saw them toiling in rowing; for the wind was contrary unto them: and about the fourth watch of the night he cometh unto them, walking upon the sea, and would have passed by them. But when they saw him walking upon the sea, they supposed it had been a spirit, and cried out: For they all saw him, and were troubled. And immediately he talked with them, and saith unto them, Be of good cheer: it is I; be not afraid. And he went up unto them into the ship; and the wind ceased: and they were sore amazed in themselves beyond measure, and wondered." (Mark 6:45-51).*

When the perfect storm was over they were *"sore amazed"*, it almost hurt to be so shocked. I imagine you would be sore amazed if it were you on the boat and saw what just happened.

Here were the men in the midst of the sea. They were not backsliding, not giving up on the Lord, and not throwing in the towel. But they were also not making any headway in life because the *"winds were contrary"* and they were *"toiling in rowing"*. Toiling is working hard and long. It appears the experienced sailors dropped their sails to avoid their being torn by the fierce winds, and switched to rowing to make some headway. They were wearing themselves out trying to fight the waves, but they were not going anywhere. Have you ever been in a situation where it seems like everything is against you?

In my teenage years, whilst living near a beach on the Sunshine Coast in Queensland, it was not an uncommon experience to be caught in a rip in the ocean whilst swimming. It is then you realise what toiling means when you try to swim against the rip. In fact many people drown from toiling in swimming in a dangerous ocean rip.

During a summer cyclone one year, I was attempting to walk home on a beachfront and was walking into the cyclonic head wind. The wind was so strong it seemed like I was making little to no progress leaning on a forty-five degree angle because the wind was contrary.

Sometimes you are toiling and rowing and going nowhere because the stormy winds of life are pushing you back and you're going nowhere fast.

Have you ever been working, then stop and look and it seems like you've gotten nowhere? It's like when you are not very hungry and are served up a plate of spaghetti. You keep on eating and it seems like you're not even making a dent in the pile of food.

Being in a storm was the will of God

The consolation in the account of the disciples toiling on the sea is knowing these men were smack dead in the middle of the will of God, because Jesus had told them to get in the boat and sail to the other side. They were right where God wanted them. In fact the Bible says that Jesus *"constrained"* them to get in the boat and start sailing. The storm came because they were in the will of God. They were safer in the storm in God's will than on land out of God's will. Many Christians think that obedience to God produces smooth sailing and to be in this kind of situation is a horrible situation to be in. We need to realise as part of the will of God, you may be in a trial; *"Beloved, think it not strange concerning the fiery trial which is to try you, as though some strange thing happened unto you: But rejoice, inasmuch as ye are partakers of Christ's sufferings; that, when his glory shall be revealed, ye may be glad also with exceeding joy."* (1 Peter 4:12-13).

We live in a day where contrary winds are never far away from us. They may come in the fashion of an unseen opposition, closed doors or even people opposing us. What we must realise is that God knows all about it. It may be we are toiling so that God can do something in us before He does something through us.

Walking on water isn't impossible, it's miraculous

Mark wrote: *"about the fourth watch of the night he cometh unto them, walking upon the sea."* Do you believe Jesus walked on water? I certainly do. I believe all the miracles of Jesus.

I'm told of an alcoholic who became a believer, and was asked how he could possibly believe all the nonsense in the Bible about miracles. "You don't believe that Jesus changed the water into wine do you?" "I sure do, because in our house Jesus changed the beer into furniture and food!"

When Jesus came walking on the water the already fearful disciples became troubled. However, there may be times where God's way of getting you to your next level comes in the form of something that scares you. Anytime God moves us up, He is moving you out of your comfort zone of service. Why does He do that? We get so comfortable in our situations and circumstances that we start living as though we don't need Him. So just about the time you get settled, God will send a storm in your life that causes you to turn back to Him.

We can wrongly assume things about God in the storms. They thought He was a spirit. They didn't recognize Jesus when He came to them. It was not like they had not seen Him in a while. They had just spent time with him and a full day had not passed. He came walking toward them and they were frightened. But isn't that just like us. We don't see Jesus in our storms? Why? We are so caught up in what we are going through that we don't recognize when God shows up. The disciples couldn't see Jesus due to the fact that their attention was on the storm that was around them.

The Lord gave great encouragement in the storm and told them to cheer up because He really was there. In Matthew's account of the incident he adds what Peter says and does in response to Jesus' walking on the water. *"And when the disciples saw him walking on the sea, they were troubled, saying, It is a spirit; and they cried out for fear. But straightway Jesus spake unto them, saying, **Be of good cheer; it is I; be not afraid**. And Peter answered him and said, Lord, if it be thou, bid me come unto thee on the water. And he said, Come. And when **Peter** was come down out of the ship, he **walked***

on the water, *to go to Jesus. (Matthew 14:26-29).*

While everyone else sat around wondering, Peter was tired of waiting. He wanted to know if there was any need for him to be scared any longer. Jesus gave a one word invitation and Peter was up and over the edge of the boat. You can just hear the other eleven disciples in the boat saying things like, "Peter, what do you think you are doing?", "Peter, get back here, are you crazy?", "Peter, we have never done that before!" "Peter, are you sure about what you're doing?"

But...

Peter placed one foot down on the water and thought, "OK that's working", and then he began to walk on water towards Jesus. Then came the ominous conjunction – "but"; *"But when he saw the wind boisterous, he was **afraid**; and beginning to sink, he cried, saying, Lord, save me. And immediately Jesus stretched forth his hand, and caught him, and said unto him, O thou of **little faith**, wherefore didst thou **doubt**? (Matthew 14:30-31).*

Sometimes I wish there were another twenty verses to describe what happened in that moment. Peter turned his gaze from the Saviour to the storm and began to sink. Then Jesus extended his arm supernaturally and pulled him to safety. As long as Peter had his eyes on the Lord he was safe and would not slip into the water. But when Peter saw the wind, he was afraid and began to sink. Fear again crept in and produced his anxious moment. Any time we take our eyes off the Lord and put them on the circumstances around us, we're going to slip!

In another panic moment Peter began to sink in that on which he should be walking. Jesus told him he was able to walk on the water and come to Him. Jesus said the reason Peter began to sink was because of his doubt; *"O thou of little faith, wherefore didst thou doubt?"*

Fear began to come into his thoughts. That fear created doubt and panic. He doubted the mighty power of God in his life. When we start to allow doubts to creep into our thought life, they become the seeds to grow fear which can produce the fruit of anxiety. This is why our thought life is crucial in moments of panic attack.

Emotions are like the warning lights on the dashboards of our cars; they indicate there is a problem under the bonnet (or hood for my American friends), a problem with our thoughts. Thoughts are the initiators; emotions are the indicators. So when I begin to have the emotion of fear and anxious thoughts I must look at what is the initiator of these emotions and thoughts. Doubting God's faithfulness, power, presence, abilities, protection and promises become thoughts that initiate the negative emotions of fear, frustration, bitterness, anger, discouragement, despair (depression), hatred, and so forth. We must strive to replace the enemy thoughts of fear/doubt. As I have already mentioned, fear and faith are both powered by focus, and through doubt Peter lost his focus. He began to be focused on the problem which created fear, doubt and anxiety eventually causing him to begin to go down. Thankfully Peter was close enough to Jesus for Him to stretch forth His hand to reach him.

The wind ceased

The story concludes with this final verse, *"And when they were come into the ship, the wind ceased."* *(Matthew 14:32)*. I'm glad to report to you that storms are always of a limited duration and Jesus is the one who can cause the wind to cease.

What winds are against you right now? What peace do you

need? Are you willing to look to Jesus who wants to come to you? Are you willing to let go of the safety of that boat you've built for yourself? Are you ready to stop the ceaseless rowing against the contrary winds of life, job and relationships...and let Jesus calm the storm in you? Reach out to Jesus, put away your doubts and cry out like Peter "Lord, save me" and trust in the Lord to take hold of you and remove your doubts.

Chapter 4

CHOKING ON WORRY

I'M ALARMED

Fear creates Worry as a source of Anxiety

Are you a world class champion worrier? If worry were an Olympic event would you be in the running for a gold medal?

We can all agree that when it comes to membership in the human race, worry is part of the package. Whether it is personal concerns, family matters, financial needs, health issues, governmental policies, or global conditions, we all have reasons to worry and fret. Sometimes critical situations strike immediate fear in our hearts, and that is only natural. However, much of our anxiety is associated with everyday problems that we end up worrying about. We wake up with our worries, carry them around all day, and then take them to bed with us.

Worry leads to fretting and fretting leads to anxiety. This is not a modern day problem or some new medical fad because we have too many 'i-devices.' It was also an issue for those who lived in Old Testament times. King David, the sweet psalmist of Israel, said, *"Rest in the LORD, and wait patiently for him: **fret not** thyself* *because of him who prospereth in his way, because of the man who bringeth wicked devices to pass. Cease from anger, and forsake wrath:* **fret not** *thyself in any wise to do evil." (Psalm 37:7-8).*

By the time the Roman Empire ruled the world, there were plenty of reasons for worry which produced an anxious nation. When Jesus came on the scene, He addressed the issue of worry and anxiety when He preached the greatest sermon of all history (found in Matthew 5-7). He was very clear on this issue of anxiety and what he said makes the solution seem so simple that we wonder why we still struggle with it.

Jesus basically asks a series of questions in His sermon when addressing anxiety to help us determine and conclude that worry is a waste of time. As you answer each of these questions it quickly becomes apparent that worrying is irrational, ineffective, inconsistent and illogical.

Consider questions like: Who of you by worrying can add a single hour to your life? Who of you by worrying can grow taller? Who of you by worrying has upgraded your wardrobe or reduced your grocery bill? Who of you by worrying has added value to what you value most? If worrying hasn't accomplished any of that for you, but has potentially weakened your life, then why worry?

Jesus says anxiety will tear you apart

In a nine-verse passage in Matthew 6:25-34, Jesus repeats the expression 'Take no thought' five times. The phrase simply means "stop being worried or anxious".

The Greek word used in this phrase is *merimnaó* which comes from the word *mérimna* which means to be separated from the whole; dividing and fracturing a person's being into parts.[12]

This phrase gives us the word picture of a divided mind. The worrier has a mind torn between the real and the possible, the present and the future, the immediate and the potential. He's trying to fight the battle of life on two fronts, and he's bound to lose the war. The worrier attempts to live in the future, and that presents him with two problems: The future isn't here, and the future isn't his. Nothing can be done, and no amount of worrying affects the issue one iota. The future is unknown, uncontrollable, and therefore irrelevant in terms of our peace of mind.

This word usage carries the idea of being drawn in opposite directions or "to go to pieces" because of being pulled apart in different directions. The first thing anxiety does to us is isolate us and separate us. That's why when you are suffering from anxiety you start feeling fragmented. You have the sensation of falling apart and think you are losing your mind. Anxiety will take you away from the people you love, from your work, from your family and your friends. It will cause you to want to run and hide. Anxiety is a separator and you are under attack.

Do the birds worry?

Problems can so easily overwhelm us that we feel insignificant and incapable of doing anything about them. It seems the complexity of life robs us of the possibility of peace. When we think about the big issues and demands of life we can often feel like God doesn't care about "little old me." Yet Jesus says to look at the birds who seem so inconsequential in the bigger scheme of life and notice how God cares for them. Jesus said *"Therefore I say unto you, **Take***

---

12 http://biblehub.com/greek/3309.htm

no thought *for your life, what ye shall eat, or what ye shall drink; nor yet for your body, what ye shall put on. Is not the life more than meat, and the body than raiment? Behold the fowls of the air: for they sow not, neither do they reap, nor gather into barns; yet your heavenly Father feedeth them. Are ye not much better than they?"* (Matthew 6:25-26).

We never see birds driving a tractor, ploughing the ground, planting seeds or harvesting crops. They are totally inadequate for that task and can't even hold a hoe or shovel. If God cares so much for them, we can be certain that He will be faithful to meet our needs as well.

This is why Jesus said not to get anxious about the provisions in life. If you believe that God is the creator of all then you must be consistent and also believe in a sustainer God or you're simply inconsistent. The detail of creation and the marvel of the human anatomy continually remind us that we have a caring creator. The evidence of His loving and timely care is all around us.

In this passage Jesus is talking to a first century audience whose main concerns of life were food, water and clothing. They are not necessarily the concerns of today. Most people in the Western world aren't worried about eating, drinking and having enough clothes. However, we still have modern day worries and concerns that consume our thinking and wonder if God is able to help us take care of our needs.

Take a moment to really ponder your worth before God and ask yourself if you need to worry whether God cares about you? Think about what Jesus said about the birds. You are much more valuable than they, and yet God knows when a sparrow falls to the ground. If God cares about a sparrow, surely He cares about you.

Just as a side note, we sometimes make fascinating discoveries when we compare two separate Scripture passages together.

Consider this matter of the value of sparrows. Matthew tells us that two sparrows are sold for a farthing (a coin worth one quarter of a penny) *"Are not **two sparrows** sold for **a farthing**? and one of them shall not fall on the ground without your Father."* *(Matthew 10:29).* Then in the Gospel of Luke we read another market value, *"Are not **five sparrows** sold for **two farthings**, and not one of them is forgotten before God?"* *(Luke 12:6).* Putting the passages together we discover from Matthew that one coin will get you two birds and from Luke that two coins will get you five, or you might say, 'buy four and get one free.' But, not even the free sparrow, which has no market value, can fall to the ground without your heavenly Father knowing about it. He follows every movement of His creation. If God is so meticulous with the smallest, most incidental creatures, won't He also tend to your deeper concerns?

Does worry make you taller?

We tend to worry and become anxious about our attempt to change things we cannot control. Jesus reminds us that many situations are beyond our ability to alter. *"Which of you by **taking thought** can add one cubit unto his stature?"* *(Matthew 6:27).* None of us can think ourselves taller; if we could it would have huge implications for basketball players!

Have you noticed that in Jesus' sermon on worry He makes reference to specific values and measurements? The reason for this is because when we deal with worry it is so easy to lose perspective of true worth. By referring to a monetary value or a height measurement (a cubit) Jesus is getting us to focus on truth and not lose perspective.

There are many circumstances in life that we cannot change and to take thought and worry over these does nothing to change them. When we try to control them we only multiply the intensity of our pain and frustration in finding out we can't control them. Worrying over matters we cannot change merely divides the mind, multiplies misery, and subtracts from our happiness, but it never adds. Someone once said, "Worry pulls tomorrow's cloud over today's sunshine."

Have you ever watched a mouse in a cage running for his life on the mouse wheel? It is thought that an average pet mouse will run fifteen thousand kilometres in his lifetime and yet he has gone nowhere. That's what worry is like; we frantically allow our thoughts to run and yet we are still stuck in the prison of our anxiety.

Interestingly, the word "worry" in ancient English means "to choke or to strangle." So when you worry, the meaning of the English word is likened to somebody who has you by your spiritual throat and is choking the life out of you. Worry is literally spiritual, mental and emotional strangulation. Whenever you give into worry, your mind can become paralysed and incapable of rational thought. It goes around and around and around like the mouse on the wheel but it doesn't go anywhere. It seems you are incapable of doing anything about it, you have the same thought going on in your mind, over and over because you have no conclusion to it. You've allowed worry to have control of your mind and it's choking you so you can't think creatively.

The flowers remind us not to worry

Jesus draws our attention to flowers and how gloriously they clothe the fields. He then reminds us that God will take care of our clothing needs as well, and it is futile to get anxious over this provision. *"And why **take ye thought** for raiment? Consider* *the lilies of the field, how they grow; they toil not, neither do they spin: And yet I say unto you, That even Solomon in all his glory was not arrayed like one of these. Wherefore, if God so clothe the grass of the field, which to day is, and to morrow is cast into the oven, shall he not much more clothe you, O ye of little faith?" (Matthew 6:28-30).* Have you ever seen a lily suffering through an anxiety attack? They neither toil nor spin but simply sway in the breeze, reaching heavenward toward the source of their water, sunshine and sustenance. It's as though they are trusting in their creator.

Our failure to trust God to provide for our needs can become a source of anxiety. When we worry that our needs won't be met, we demonstrate a lack of faith in God. Part of our problem is that we don't know what our needs truly are. Advertising does a great job in helping us confuse our wants with our needs.

God values you so much more than a flower which He created merely for His and our pleasure. So, if God cares for each petal or stem that blooms and fades within a season, how much more does He care for you? How much more does He take to heart the things that cause your anxiety? We find the answer to those questions when we cast our mind to the cross of Calvary two thousand years ago. It was there that God displayed His love and care for you.

Do you trust that God can and will take care of you? Here is the central issue of worry and anxiety. Worry is a failure to trust in God. Look at the creation of God and recognise how big He is and how important are you, *"O ye of little faith."*

Make God your priority

In making some summary remarks on worry, Jesus tells us to focus on His priorities rather than our own in order to avoid becoming anxious. He tells us not to worry about what we "shall:

eat, drink or wear" in the future, but rather live today with a trust and confidence in God who knows what we need. *"Therefore **take no thought**, saying, What **shall** we eat? or, What **shall** we drink? or, Wherewithal **shall** we be clothed? (For after all these things do the Gentiles seek:) for your heavenly Father **knoweth** that ye have need of all these things. But seek ye first the kingdom of God, and his righteousness; and all these things shall be added unto you." (Matthew 6:31-33).* When we make it our top priority to acknowledge Him as our Lord and Saviour, seeking to walk obediently in His ways, God promises to supply whatever else we need. He knows exactly what is best for us, as well as how and when to provide it. What if you could live with an absolute confidence and abiding certainty that God KNOWS what you need? Wouldn't that help to eliminate worry and anxiety?

When we boil it all down, worry is about seeking after things in the future. Worry is all about chasing things mentally, chasing things emotionally, seeking after things and trying to control the outcomes. That's what people who have no confidence in God do. But those who put God first put their trust and confidence in God to control the future.

Finally Jesus tells us to let tomorrow's problems wait until tomorrow. Trying to live tomorrow today will only end in more anxiety. *"**Take therefore no thought** for the morrow: for the morrow shall **take thought** for the things of itself. Sufficient unto the day is the evil thereof." (Matthew 6:34).* Planning ahead is good, but sometimes our overloaded calendars lead to an overwhelming sense of time pressure. Instead of becoming anxious about our responsibilities and commitments, we should turn our schedules over to God. When you're tempted to borrow from tomorrow, look for a way to participate in what God is doing today and trust Him for tomorrow. Don't smuggle tomorrow's trouble into today because Jesus says today has enough trouble of its own, *"Sufficient unto the day is the evil thereof."*

Jesus says don't worry because your heavenly Father is with you today and He will be waiting on you tomorrow. Stop magnifying problems and minimizing God, and start magnifying God and minimizing the problems.

Being a pastor for the last twenty years and meeting and counselling with numerous people, I have come to realise that some people will not believe that God is there for them. They will argue and give three general reasons why they don't decide to trust in an invisible God. They would claim the concept is absurd; they are not sure it will "work"; and they are not sure God will come through for them.

However if you chose not to place your faith in your heavenly Father, essentially you are placing your faith in worry! Now here is the question: which one is more dependable, worry or your heavenly Father?

Imagine if I replaced the word "worry" for the word "LORD" in my wife's favourite Scripture. It would read like this, *"Trust in WORRY with all thine heart; and lean not unto thine own understanding. In all thy ways acknowledge WORRY, and WORRY shall direct thy paths." (Proverbs 3:5-6).*

Imagine that the premise of this book is to put your faith in worry. You'd say, "The concept is absurd; I know that doesn't work; and worry never comes through for me."

Think about it, no-one ever sings songs about trusting worry!

Some questions to consider

What kinds of situations or issues cause you to worry or feel anxious? Do you tend to worry more about what's happening now, or what could happen in the future? What changes do you need to make in your thought patterns, activities, and prayers in order to be free from worry?

For many people, worry becomes so ingrained in their personalities that, once the old worries are gone, they search for new ones. They've become dependent on worry as a lens through which to view life, and they've forgotten any other way to live. Do you want to become that kind of person? I know I don't.

The challenge lies in placing our full confidence in God as we face the things that breed worry in our lives. We choose to either worry or to trust God. That isn't always an easy choice.

J. Arthur Rank was one of the early pioneers of the film industry in Great Britain, and he also happened to be a devout Christian. Rank found he couldn't push his worries out of his mind completely; they were always slipping back in. So he finally made a pact with God to limit his worrying to Wednesday. He even made himself a little Wednesday Worry Box and he placed it on his desk. Whenever a worry cropped up, Rank wrote it out and dropped it into the Wednesday Worry Box. When Wednesday rolled around, he would open that box to find that only a third of the items he had written down were still worth worrying about. The rest had managed to resolve themselves.

Will you choose to trust or will you choose to worry?

Part 2

THE SOLUTIONS FOR ANXIETY

Chapter 5

TURN CARE INTO PRAYER

I HAVE ACCESS

Faith accesses prayer as a solution to anxiety

Chained in a rat-infested Roman prison doesn't sound like a great place to be rejoicing? To the contrary, it seems to be the place you resign to be miserable. But not so for the apostle Paul. He takes quill and ink and records another wonderful letter expounding on all the reasons he has to rejoice, and encourages the readers at Philippi to live in peace, not panic.

The word "peace" brings different responses from different people. Some think of world peace. Others may think of a hippy's peace. Maybe to parents it is the sound of silence when the children are finally all asleep in bed. We think peace is the absence of conflict and stress. Therefore, when we are praying for peace we are requesting God for a change in our circumstances, but that is not what God is talking about. He is able to give us peace right in the midst of the stressful times and pressures of life. It is an internal peace that strengthens and stabilises us, no matter what is happening around us. Jesus said, "*Peace I leave with you, my peace*

I give unto you: not as the world giveth, give I unto you. Let not your heart be troubled, neither let it be afraid." (John 14:27).

God's definition of peace is not the absence of something, it is the presence of someone – Him!

Wouldn't it be great to be able to say, "I don't have anything to worry about today; everything in my life is in order." It would be like Timon and Pumbaa's catch phrase in the movie, 'The Lion King', "Hakuna Matata!" (A Swahili phrase from Kenya that literally means "no worries.") But it doesn't happen very often, does it?

I once read a letter from a stressed-out friend that described himself in the prison of stress and anxiety. Part of the letter reads as follows:

My Life stinks! How's the family? I'm OK, really I am but don't touch me or I'll have to kill you! As you can probably tell from the preceding, everything is pretty normal around here. The air conditioning doesn't work; the car is just hanging on, having only required a new clutch and brake job; the washing machine fell apart; the hard drive on my computer crashed; the door fell off the dishwasher; and we a have a hot water leak (you can hear it running, but we can't find it!) That is just in the last month. I know someone's bound to have it worse than me (I pity the fool) but occasionally I think Job in the Bible had it easy. Today I decided to write down a list of things that are causing me stress, thinking that if I put them down on paper they may not seem so bad…I quit at number 17; it stressed me out."

How are your stress levels? Are you stressed out and allowing fear to breed worry and doubt leading to anxiety? Paul has some great Biblical advice to help with the cares of life that are leaving you ready to quit at your number 17.

Do you Enjoy life or Endure life?

I've discovered that most people really don't enjoy life; they endure it. Their lives are filled with anxiety, stress, and pressure, but there's very little joy.

I remember reading about road rage in Los Angeles in 1994 when the three-time Oscar winning actor, Jack Nicholson, enraged at being cut off by a man in a Mercedes, jumped out of his car at the next traffic light and smashed the Benz's roof and windshield with a golf club. Ironically, years later, in 2003, Nicholson played the part of a therapist counselling Adam Sandler in the comedy movie called 'Anger Management'. Charges were dropped after Nicholson apologized to Robert Blank, the driver of the vehicle, and the two reached a settlement, which included a reported $500,000 payment from Nicholson. Nicholson later expressed regret about the incident in an interview with US Magazine, calling it "a shameful incident in my life." He explained that a close friend had recently died, and that **he had also been under a good deal of stress** during the shooting of a movie. He said - "I was on my way to the course, and in the midst of this madness I somehow knew what I was doing," he says, "because I reached into my trunk and specifically selected a club I never used on the course: my two-iron."[13]

Worry is assuming responsibility that God never intended for us to have, and of all the joy-stealers that can plague our lives, none is more nagging, more agitating or more prevalent than worry.

A study done by Dr. Walter Calvert, funded by the National Science Foundation, revealed some startling statistics about

---

13 http://articles.latimes.com/1994-03-01/local/me-28564_1_golf-club

human beings and worry. Here's what he found:

- 40% of the things we worry about never happen
- 30% of our worries are about events in the past
- 12% of our worries are unfounded health concerns
- 10% of our worries are over minor and trivial issues
- Only 8% of our worries are real, legitimate issues[14]

This study supports what Paul was teaching us when he devoted four verses to this subject in writing to the Philippians about how to overcome anxiety. Thankfully he gave us a sure fire faith remedy to deal with anxiety. He diagnosed the problem, prescribed the cure, recommended a strategy and made a comforting promise of gaining peace instead of panic. He wrote, *"Rejoice in the Lord alway: and again I say, Rejoice. Let your moderation be known unto all men. The Lord is at hand.* **Be careful for nothing; but in every thing by prayer** *and supplication with thanksgiving let your requests be made known unto God. And the peace of God, which passeth all understanding, shall keep your hearts and minds through Christ Jesus."* *(Philippians 4:4-7).*

In summary his advice is "Worry about nothing, pray about everything and thank God for anything." However, some worriers choose to turn around the adage, "Why worry when you can pray" to say, "Why pray when you can worry." In reality worry is negative mediation that robs you of peace. Worry is like prayer in reverse. The more you worry the bigger the problem seems. The more you pray the smaller the problem seems. This is why we must turn our care into prayer.

Let's consider in more detail what these four scripture verses in Philippians teach us about overcoming anxiety. God gives us the cure for care and how we can live with the peace of God guarding

---

14 http://activerain.com/blogsview/30070/don-t-worry-about-it-

our thoughts and emotions.

Rejoice in the Lord at all times through Praise

There is great joy in being a Christian and having access to all that God provides for us. This is why Paul begins his remedial advice with this admonition, *"Rejoice in the Lord alway: and again I say, Rejoice." (Philippians 4:4).* Throughout the book of Philippians there is a reoccurring theme exhorting the reader to have joy. Coincidentally there are forty references to Jesus Christ in the 104 verses of this epistle. The clear message to us is that Jesus is the reason for joy, because He is always in control no matter what the circumstances may seem.

Remain Calm and remember the Promises of God

Because we have joy in the Lord, we don't have to lash out at people and allow our fears and worries to lead us to become full of care and anxiety. Paul's instruction is to *"Let your **moderation** be known unto all men. The Lord is at hand." (Philippians 4:5).* Anxiety creates an imbalance in our thinking whereby we can move into extreme thought patterns and actions. The Christian is to pursue moderation, which means keeping a balance between extremes or excesses and having a calmness of mind. The balance is part of the cure. To not go to an extreme means we don't allow ourselves to be polarised with one aspect of our life and become anxious. We must learn to balance and be moderate as we live with the promise of the second coming of Jesus as a motivating factor to help us take stock of our life and live in moderation because *"The Lord is at hand."*

However, some will say that it is all well and good to expect the Christian to rejoice at all times and to live moderately and avoid becoming elevated in anxious moods, but how do we do that? This is where Paul prescribes the Biblical medicine to take.

Rest in the Lord and turn Care into Prayer

Whenever God tells us to eliminate something, He always has something superior to replace it, and this passage of Scripture reveals nothing less. It is simply: **replace care with prayer.** *"Be careful for nothing; but in every thing by prayer and supplication with thanksgiving let your requests be made known unto God." (Philippians 4:6).* Paul is saying, 'Don't panic – pray!'

The word 'careful' is a compound word meaning 'full of care' which plainly indicates 'worry' and is what is cautioned against by the apostle. He is literally saying, "Be careful for NO thing." To be careful or anxious is not worrying about what *has* happened, but worrying about what *might* happen in the future. So many people are stuck in anxiety because they are crippled by a possibility - a threat. It hasn't occurred yet but it might as well have because it is robbing them of peace as though it had already happened.

Anxiety is part of spiritual warfare in the Christian life. People are terrorised by thoughts of 'what if?' and 'Suppose this or that happens, what then?' They listen to the voice of terror and are gripped by fear which opens the door to anxiety and robs them of their peace. There is not one thing that God wants us to be so consumed about that we forfeit our peace. We must understand that in the war on our soul the devil doesn't want our house, he wants our peace. He doesn't want our job promotion, he wants our peace. His tactic is to do whatever it takes to rob us of peace. Jesus warned us, *"The thief cometh not, but for to **steal**, and to **kill**, and* to **destroy**: *I am come that they might have life, and that they might have it more abundantly." (John 10:10).*

I want to be sure to clarify the misuse of this verse. We must realise to *"be careful for nothing"* does not mean to not be concerned. There is a big difference between being "careful" and being "concerned." If you do show concern about your children playing near traffic, you're a responsible parent. If you're not concerned about little children playing with fire unsupervised, then you would be a neglectful parent. There are things you need to be concerned about that are genuine concerns, but don't let them become needless cares. Realistic concern and restless anxiety are separate matters. The major difference between the two, is that concern tends to focus on the present whilst anxious care and worry is attached to the future. The present is before us, and there are actions we can take. The future is out of our hands. We can turn a genuine concern into a care by allowing fear to create worry which leads to anxiety. It is okay to have concerns and to pray about them, but it's not okay to become full of care over the issue. In Philippians 4:6, Paul is referring to the captivity of carefulness that ensnares people and can propel them into a panic attack.

The tendency in life is to expect the worst, which increases worry and in turn produces carefulness. Worry cannot change the past or control the future but prayer can change many things. Prayer is a Biblical practice that puts faith ahead of fear. When Paul wrote to the Philippians he was in prison waiting to be executed by Nero, the insane Caesar of Rome. I believe he had good reason to worry, but instead he chose to pray. Paul gives us four phases in our praying to reduce anxiety.

The first is **Adoration** referred to as "prayer" in the passage. This simply means to spend time worshipping and adoring God in prayer, or as Jesus began His famous 'Lord's prayer", He said,

*"When ye pray, say, Our Father which art in heaven, **Hallowed** be thy name." (Luke 11:2).* Beginning our prayer with a moment of praise to God for Who He is and What He does, refocuses our minds on the One who is totally competent to deal with our anxiety. Prayer resolves the anxiety-provoking question of, "How shall I cope?" by redirecting our attention away from the care to God's person and promises.

Secondly we move to **Approaching** God humbly with a petition or "supplication", which is the action of asking or begging for something earnestly. Supplication is in the prayer family. It has the idea of lowering ourselves before God in humility acknowledging that what we are dealing with is too much for us and that we need God's help and intervention. When King Solomon offered up prayer and supplication he was on his knees before the Lord with his hands raised in worshipful surrender to Him, *"And it was so, that when Solomon had made an end of **praying** all this **prayer** and **supplication** unto the LORD, he arose from before the altar of the LORD, from **kneeling on his knees with his hands spread up** to heaven." (1 Kings 8:54).*

The apostle John wrote to encourage us to remember when we petition God according to His will that God is listening to our supplications, *"And this is the confidence that we have in him, that, if we ask any thing according to his will, he heareth us: And if we know that he hear us, whatsoever we **ask**, we know that we have the **petitions** that we desired of him." (1 John 5:14-15).*

The Bible includes many prayers of supplication for mercy, deliverance, forgiveness and so on. If there were ever a time to make supplication it is when we are overwhelmed with worry and in a dire strait. Daniel was in a terrible predicament facing the king's edict not to pray or he would be thrown into the lions' den. It was in this stressful moment Daniel knew his only recourse was to offer prayers and supplications to God. His enemies knew what type of man Daniel was and caught him doing just that, *"Then these men assembled, and found Daniel praying and **making supplication** before his God." (Daniel 6:11)*. Approaching God through supplications, humbly and earnestly begging God to protect and intervene in our situation is one of the greatest sources of help to reduce or remove anxiety.

The advice to overcome anxiety is to bring everything to God in *"prayer and supplication."* Always remember there is no problem that is too big for God's power or too small for God's concern. *"Ah Lord GOD! behold, thou hast made the heaven and the earth by thy great power and stretched out arm, and **there is nothing too hard for thee:" (Jeremiah 32:17)*. Don't ever be afraid to get very specific when talking to the Lord in prayer. Many people pray in general terms and vaguely ask, "God, bless my life." Instead, we need to pray very specific prayers and supplications like, *"God, I'm under stress. I'm tense, I'm nervous. Please help me rid myself of this carefulness and worry by increasing my faith in You."*

Release the anxiety by turning it into prayer. Trust the process even though you can't see it working. That is why Jesus and others continue to encourage us not to quit, and to keep praying: *"And he spake a parable unto them to this end, that men ought **always to pray**, and **not to faint**;" (Luke 18:1)*.

Lastly, we are given a final piece of the prayer puzzle, **Appreciation**. Make all of your requests and prayers in the form of *"thanksgiving"*. Have an attitude of gratitude in your life, especially in times of anxiety. You release the anxiety by turning it into gratitude. When you offer thanksgiving prayers to God you are saying, "I'm thankful you are in charge." When you let God rule and have control in your life, then the peace of God comes in, and takes over. It is through thankfulness that this exchange takes place. *"And let the **peace of God** rule in your hearts, to the which also ye are called in one body; and **be ye thankful**." (Colossians 3:15).* We gain peace in thanking God and recognising the things He has done. Live with the mindset that you are too grateful to be anxious. Spend time thanking God and praising Him for His blessings. As the old hymn writer wrote,

When upon life's billows you are tempest tossed,
When you are discouraged, thinking all is lost,
Count your many blessings, name them one by one,
And it will surprise you what the Lord hath done.

Refrain:
Count your blessings, name them one by one;
Count your blessings, see what God hath done;
Count your blessings, name them one by one;
Count your many blessings, see what God hath done.

Are you ever burdened with a load of care?
Does the cross seem heavy you are called to bear?
Count your many blessings, ev'ry doubt will fly,
And you will be singing as the days go by.[15]

Ungrateful people also tend to be unhappy people. If you are anxious take time to make a list of fifty things you can be thankful for. Thanksgiving will become like a safety valve that releases pressure.

Now that your attitude is right and you're not approaching God in a state of panic, you can now make your requests known unto Him. You have spent time Adoring, Approaching and

---

15 http://library.timelesstruths.org/music/Count_Your_Blessings/

Appreciating God, and Paul says now **Ask** God for your requests. *"Be careful for nothing; but in every thing by prayer and supplication with thanksgiving* **let your requests be made known unto God.***" (Philippians 4:6).* There is a difference between intellectually wrapping your mind around this verse, and personalising this verse and believing it. We are given the opportunity to bring our requests directly to God. Doctors are helpful, but I'm glad I can make requests to the great physician Himself. When I do this, at that moment what was stressing me is now sitting in the hands of God. There is a divine interaction and I no longer need to be full of care because I have TOLD GOD about it! Pause right now as you are reading this and ponder the magnitude of what happens when you pray like this – You just TOLD GOD in heaven your requests.

We must always remember, that whilst prayer is a comfort in uneasy times and a mighty warrior against worry, it does not automatically mean that when we pray, all the things we worry about will be straightened out for us and that our trouble will be gone. In fact, prayer may not make the situation better or change the outward circumstances that are causing the anxiety. However, prayer always changes us and makes us better. Prayer and supplications, accompanied with thanksgiving, is the perfect answer to a heart that is overridden with anxiety.

Faith in God defeats anxiety

Faith enables us to bring our requests to a God, whom we know loves us personally with an everlasting love. *"The LORD hath appeared of old unto me, saying, Yea, I have loved thee with an everlasting love: therefore with lovingkindness have I drawn thee." (Jeremiah 31:3).*

Faith equips us to come to a God whom we know will wisely do what is best for us and give us an expected end with His peace in your mind. *"For I know the thoughts that I think toward you, saith the LORD, thoughts of peace, and not of evil, to give you an expected end." (Jeremiah 29:11).*

Faith assures us that the God we are praying to is the One Who desires to grant us 'grace to help in time of need' and help us in our infirmities. *"For this thing I besought the Lord thrice, that it might depart from me. And he said unto me, My grace is sufficient for thee: for my strength is made perfect in weakness. Most gladly therefore will I rather glory in my infirmities, that the power of Christ may rest upon me. Therefore I take pleasure in infirmities, in reproaches, in necessities, in persecutions, in distresses for Christ's sake: for when I am weak, then am I strong." (2 Corinthians 12:8-10).*

We need a Peace that only God can give

Then comes the amazing result of refusing to be careful. Taking everything that is troubling us to God is the way in which He grants His peace. Paul tells us the flow-on effect of verses 4-6; *"And the peace of God, which passeth all understanding, shall keep your hearts and minds through Christ Jesus." (Philippians 4:7).* The word "keep" is a military term. It means a sentry guard, a garrison, or a detachment of soldiers that is protecting a city or place. (Paul used the word that he knew everybody would understand.) That's the way God will guard the heart and mind of all who have a relationship with Jesus Christ, and trust Him moment by moment. God will protect us with His peace from a nervous breakdown. His peace will guard us from suicidal thoughts[16] and hold us back from quitting and throwing the towel in. It is not because we are personally strong, it's because we are being kept by the God of

---

16 If you ever have suicidal thoughts you should seek help immediately.

peace.

The type of peace that I am referring to is God's peace - perfect peace that allows us to sleep peacefully, calms our troubled heart and eliminates the physical side effects of anxiety. We can't even get our mind around this peace because it *"passeth all understanding."*

Knowing that we made it all the way to God and told him our requests enables His peace to come and stand guard at the door of our heart and mind. When anxiety comes knocking at the door of our soul, the peace of God says, "Hello, what is that you're trying to bring in here? Fear? I'm sorry; no entry allowed!"

What is so calming to remember is this - the circumstances that brought the anxiety may not change; but peace doesn't come when our circumstances change. Peace comes when our requests reach God.

Chapter 6

THINK ON THESE THINGS

I CAN ASSIMILATE

Faith based Thinking is a solution to Anxiety

After teaching us how to rid ourselves of anxiety through prayer and supplication with thanksgiving, the apostle Paul moves quickly to a vital part of being able to continue being careful for nothing. He taught the Biblical principle of replacement. This entails deliberately replacing anxious thoughts with those that are more honourable, positive and healthy, which will immediately have a beneficial effect. He wrote about our thought life and told his readers, *"Finally, brethren, whatsoever things are true, whatsoever things are honest, whatsoever things are just, whatsoever things are pure, whatsoever things are lovely, whatsoever things are of good report; if there be any virtue, and if there be any praise, **think on these things**." (Philippians 4:8).*

As a pastor, I can recall the numerous times I have prescribed this verse of scripture as the mental and emotional medicine for people dealing with worry and anxiety. I personally believe Philippians 4:8 to be one of the most important verses in the Bible.

From my pastoral, counselling and personal experience dealing with my wife's mental illness and panic attacks, I have gained an understanding of the thoughts which typically can occupy people's minds. What one thinks, means more than anything else in their life. In some respects, where you are today in life is a direct result of yesterday's thinking. In other words, your tomorrow will often be determined by your thought life today. Under the inspiration of God, the wise King Solomon gave sagely advice on thinking when he wrote: *"For as he thinketh in his heart, so is he…" (Proverbs 23:7)*. It has been well said that "You are not what you think you are, but what you think, you are."[17]

Only you and God know what the thoughts of your heart are. Others only discover what is possibly going on inside of you as they observe your actions and your attitudes. Your thoughts and the actions that they trigger, determine your whole life, because your mind is extraordinarily powerful. Your thoughts can make you feel powerful or powerless, a victim or a victor, a hero or a coward. They can raise or lower your heart rate, improve or interfere with your digestion, change the chemical composition of your blood, and help you to sleep or keep you awake at night.[18]

God tells us there is a great connection between our thinking and how stressed we are, *"Thou wilt keep him in perfect peace, whose mind is stayed on thee: because he trusteth in thee." (Isaiah 26:3)*. To reduce the unhealthy effects of stress in your life you must change the way you think. Stress is an internal response which is affected by external triggers. The stress is inside yourself not outside. No matter what you are facing or how difficult things may seem to be, even if you are wondering why God has allowed you to be in the situation you are in, if you purposefully let your mind dwell on

17 http://www.azquotes.com/quote/839907
18 https://patch.com/massachusetts/concord/bp

positive, uplifting thoughts they will enable you to survive.

It's a Battle for the Mind

The mind is like an amazing computer that God put in between our ears. It is so programmable and impressionable that there is a constant war between good and evil for the code to program our mind. Paul called it a war in our mind, *"But I see another law in my members, warring against the law of my mind, and bringing me into captivity to the law of sin which is in my members." (Romans 7:23).* It's a strategic battlefield where both the devil and God are fighting as to who gets into our data base and to program our mind. To overcome anxiety we must practice mind renewal. This is what thought replacement is all about. Paul said, *"And be not conformed to this world: but be ye transformed by the **renewing of your mind**, that ye may prove what is that good, and acceptable, and perfect, will of God." (Romans 12:2).*

The key to changing our life and gaining victory over anxiety is to change the way we think. The Scripture teaches that the way we think determines the way we feel, and the way we feel determines the way we act. Most people try to change themselves by changing the way they feel or the way they act, rather than going to the source and changing the way they think. We cannot change the way we feel. Feelings don't respond well to commands. We can't command a feeling, but we can change the way we think which will change the way we feel. Feelings cannot be controlled, but the source of feelings can and that is how you think. All change starts in your thought life and true transformation takes place in the mind. We must allow the Holy Spirit to renew the mind through the Word of God and right thinking, *"And be **renewed** in the spirit of your **mind**;" (Ephesians 4:23).*

Reflect on the Lord at all times through 'Right Thinking'

In the passage to the Philippians Paul uses the word *"think"* which is the Greek word *logizesthe*, meaning "to ponder, to consider, to give proper weight and value to, to meditate upon." The apostle gave the Philippians eight filters for proper meditation and thought. If we apply faith-based thinking following these guidelines, we will have victory in our battle to overcoming anxiety and panic attacks.

Follow the eight Guidelines from verse 8

In preparation to deal with wrong thinking it is advisable to take the eight thought guidelines and write down a list of areas to think upon that match the scriptural admonitions.

Guideline one: Think on the Real not the Phony - *"whatsoever things are **true**...think on these things."* In times of mental anguish and anxiety, true, real, genuine and sincere thoughts should be your number one priority. In the Bible there are several things that are referred to as "true." The Word of God itself is a worthy source of true thoughts. Jesus said, *"Sanctify them through thy truth: thy word is truth." (John 17:17)*. Bible memorisation is a good practice to aid you in thinking on things that are true. When you ponder on the truth it will not be long before the falsehood of wrong beliefs embraced in your mind will be challenged. Jesus said, *"And ye shall know the truth, and the truth shall make you free." (John 8:32)*. We must keep in mind that Satan is a liar and wants to corrupt our minds with his lies, as he has successfully accomplished in the past. Paul warned *"But I fear, lest by any means, as the serpent beguiled*

Eve through his subtilty, so your minds should be corrupted from the simplicity that is in Christ. (2 Corinthians 11:3).

Guideline two: Think on Respectful things not Corrupt things - *"whatsoever things are **honest**...think on these things."* Honesty is a rare virtue and should be sought after and practiced, especially among Christians. The opposite of honesty is dishonesty and you need to stay away from any activities that go against the principles of God's Word giving them no thought. We are to think on things that are honourable, things that claim respect and live a life worthy of God, praying that *"we may lead a quiet and peaceable life in all godliness and **honesty**. (1 Timothy 2:2).*

Guideline three: Think on what is Right not just Convenient - *"whatsoever things are **just**...think on these things."* There are many temptations within the world to be unjust thus drawing Christians after them. One temptation is to do what is easiest and convenient, even though it may not be honourable before God. Some people live by the motto, 'the end justifies the means.' This is not how God sees it. If it is unlawful, unholy, and unjust, then the Christian should not be thinking about it or indulging in it. We are to think on things that are just, which means things that are upright, righteous, faultless, and guiltless. Paul told us to guard our mind and focus on things that are just and righteous by both divine and human standards.

Guideline four: Think on things that are Clean as opposed to Impure - *"whatsoever things are **pure**...think on these things."* Living in the impure environment of Philippi, the Philippians were encouraged to fill their minds with pure thoughts in order to combat the unclean influences in their culture. Life today is no different. It seems everything you hear, tune into, click open or log onto, makes the quest for purity a challenging one. I am sure that pornography quickly comes to mind, but while it is one aspect of that which is 'not clean,' there are many other 'unclean' things that fit the bill that ought not to occupy our minds, such as envious and covetous thoughts. The greatest way to stay clean is by heeding God's Word, *"Wherewithal shall a young man cleanse his way? by taking heed thereto according to thy word." (Psalm 119:9).* This thought pattern strengthens you spiritually, and is the opposite of filthiness, foolish talking, and coarse jesting as cautioned against by Paul, *"Neither filthiness, nor foolish talking, nor jesting, which are not convenient: but rather giving of thanks." (Ephesians 5:4).* The second coming of Jesus is also a motivator to stay pure before God, *"And every man that hath this hope in him **purifieth** himself, even as he is **pure**." (1 John 3:3).*

Guideline five: Think on things that are Loving not Hateful - *"whatsoever things are **lovely**…think on these things."* Once again the perfect person to give heed to in our thoughts is the lovely Lord Jesus Himself. Solomon prophetically describes Him this way, *"His mouth is most sweet: yea, **he is altogether lovely**. This is my beloved, and this is my friend, O daughters of Jerusalem." (Song of Solomon 5:16).* Besides the Lord, what should fill our mind are thoughts of things, events and people that are acceptable, pleasing, winsome and amiable. Ezekiel spoke of music that was lovely and pleasant, *"And, lo, thou art unto them as a very **lovely song** of one that hath a **pleasant voice**, and can **play well on an instrument**:" (Ezekiel 33:32).* Listening to some *"lovely"* worship music is helpful in fixing our minds on our *"lovely"* Lord Jesus.

Guideline six: Think on things that Build up not Tear down
- *"whatsoever things are of **good report**...think on these things."*
The words *"good report"* describe that which is appealing, highly regarded, well thought of and well sounding. It is easy to be critical in our thinking. We need to think on things that build up not destroy other people's character or reputations. Think about people and events that bring good news and avoid murmuring against others with your mouth or in your thoughts, *"Do all things without murmurings and disputings:" (Philippians 2:14)*. When Joshua and Caleb came back from their spy mission to the Promised Land, they focused on the good report not the evil report. They were not denying the existence of the giants and obstacles, rather, they focused on the size of God and the good things He had given into their hands: *"And Joshua the son of Nun, and Caleb the son of Jephunneh, which were of them that searched the land, rent their clothes: And they spake unto all the company of the children of Israel, saying, The land, which we passed through to search it, is an **exceeding good** land. If the LORD **delight in us**, then he will bring us into this land, and **give it us**; a land which **floweth** with milk and honey. Only rebel not ye against the LORD, neither fear ye the people of the land; for they are **bread for us**: their defence is departed from them, and the **LORD is with us**: fear them not. (Numbers 14:6-9).*

Guideline seven: Think on things of Excellence rather than the Inferior - *"if there be any **virtue**...think on these things."* The word *"virtue"* means moral goodness; and in particular moral excellence as found in modesty, morality and motivation for us to do better. We must be cautious in our choices of movies we watch, internet sites we visit, music we listen to, books and magazines we read, etc. Ask yourself, "Does it promote morality, decency and virtuousness?" If not, then avoid it and don't let it influence your thinking. In addition to this, it is beneficial to think on things that are done with excellence rather than allow our thoughts to dwell on inferior things; such as projects that have failed or matters that have little to no value to God. We must guard ourselves from becoming fault finders and instead, notice and look for the excellence around us.

Guideline eight: Think on the Positive not the Negative - *"if there be any **praise**...think on these things."* In other words, if it is praiseworthy it is worth repeating for the benefit and edification of others. Oftentimes anxious thoughts are based in insecurities of what people think about us or our circumstances. They can also stem from negative meditation on what other people have said or done. When we take these negative thoughts and replace them with edifying praiseworthy thoughts, these insecurities vanish.

Each of Paul's thought ingredients are explicitly positive and we become responsible to choose these types of thoughts. We all have the option to choose a thought program which will produce either a Christian mind or a carnal mind. The consequences of the choices we make are unmistakable, *"For to be **carnally minded** is death; but to be **spiritually minded** is life and peace. Because the **carnal mind** is enmity against God: for it is not subject to the law of God, neither indeed can be."* (Romans 8:6).

Our thought life is the key to maintaining sanity and avoiding anxiety because both fear and faith are products of our focus. When we focus on the wrong things, fear is produced. But when we focus on the right things, faith is produced. An unfocused mind welcomes fear and weakens faith. For example, in the Garden of Eden, God told Adam he could eat all he wanted of any tree in the garden, except the Tree of the Knowledge of Good and Evil.

Things would have been much different if Adam and Eve had focused on what they could eat instead of on what they couldn't. In the same way, instead of focusing on not thinking wrong thoughts, we need to focus on thinking right thoughts. This is why the eight guidelines from Philippians 4:8 are crucial to anxiety-free living. We must learn to hold to the right Biblical thoughts and to make captive the thoughts that attempt to take hold of us, *"bringing into captivity every thought to the obedience of Christ;" (2 Corinthians 10:5).*

Check your thoughts

How we think affects the way we feel; the way we feel affects the way we act. This is why we must check all our thoughts by the reference point of how Jesus would think. WWJD has been a Christian motivation acronym printed on all manner of apparel and accessories to remind the wearer to ask "What Would Jesus Do?" if He were in my shoes. We could add to this WWJT prompting us to ask, "What Would Jesus Think?"

The masterful writer of most of the New Testament, the apostle Paul, tells us that we have divine weapons that have the power to destroy every argument and pretension raised against the thoughts of God. He gave us the charge to take every thought captive and obey Christ. He instructs us to each capture our own thoughts and examine them according to whether they match up to how Jesus would think. In encouraging us to fight a good fight and win in the thought battle in our mind, Paul gives us our Biblical thinking warfare strategy when he said, *"For though we walk in the flesh, we do not war after the flesh: (For the weapons of our warfare are not carnal, but mighty through God to the pulling down of strong holds;) Casting down **imaginations**, and every **high thing that exalteth*** *itself against the knowledge of God, and **bringing into captivity** **every thought** to the obedience of Christ; And having in a readiness to revenge all disobedience, when your obedience is fulfilled." (2 Corinthians 10:3-6).*

Spiritual warfare is a battle for the minds of people who are captive to lies that are exalted in opposition to the Word of God. They can be useless reasoning, worldly humanistic wisdom, anti-biblical ideologies, false religions, as well as our own insecurities and preconceived ideas. Many of the lies we believe are what create the fear which leads to anxiety. We must pull these strongholds down and replace them with Biblical thinking.

We can't always control the thoughts we have, but we can control the thoughts we hold. Some thoughts come from God, some come from the enemy, and some come from our own thinking. We need to learn how to hold the thoughts that are true, honest, just, pure, lovely, of a good report, having virtue or worthy of praise.

In bringing our thoughts into captivity we need to screen each one and establish if it complies with the eight guidelines. Many thoughts are dispatched by Satan to terrorize our faith like fiery darts shot from the bow of an enemy archer. However, God has given us a shield made specifically and intentionally to extinguish those fiery darts – the shield of faith: *"Above all, taking the shield of faith, wherewith ye shall be able to quench all the fiery darts of the wicked." (Ephesians 6:16).* Belief that God is greater than the enemy and that He will equip you to overcome this assault on your mind is how we hold up the shield of faith. – *"I sought the LORD, and he heard me, and delivered me from all my fears." (Psalm 34:4).*

Paul tells us what to do with these types of oppressive thoughts. God requires us to interrogate them and destroy them by casting them down and thinking on the eight godly thought guidelines. But first we need to identify the enemy thoughts. We can't shoot at an enemy we don't recognise. What do our anxious thoughts look like? Here are some practical steps to help find out:

- Keep a running list of "if only" thoughts and "what if" thoughts."
- Add to the list any recurring thoughts of doubt and uncertainties. Remember, our thoughts can scare us. What do the "monsters under your bed" look like?
- Keep a journal of upsets to track the times during the day or evening we are most plagued with the "enemy" thoughts of anxiety.
- Then search the scriptures for what God says about these thoughts and ask WWJT? Meditate on these things.

Reject your "enemy thoughts" of anxiety.

Throughout the Bible there are 366 commands from God telling us to *"fear not"*. If the Lord commands us to do this then it is entirely possible to do it. Even if life seems overwhelming, we must corral every thought and bring it into obedience to Christ choosing not to be afraid by standing on promises like this one, *"**Fear thou not**; for I am with thee: **be not dismayed**; for I am thy God: I will strengthen thee; yea, I will help thee; yea, I will uphold thee with the right hand of my righteousness."*

We are told not to fear and not to be dismayed. To be dismayed means to have sudden or complete loss of courage; utter disheartenment as by sudden danger or trouble; to become disillusioned. We need to be aware that 'fear' and 'dismay' are the two enemies that will keep us from overcoming anxiety. They are the two things that will cause us to miss our destiny because fear keeps us from starting, and discouragement keeps us from finishing what we have started.

When we break this verse down into its parts we discover an encouraging truth. Read the verse again with emphasis on the highlighted words, *"**Fear thou not**; for **I am** with thee: **be not dismayed**; for **I am** thy God: **I will** strengthen thee; **yea, I will** help thee; **yea, I will** uphold thee with the right hand of my righteousness."* *(Isaiah 41:10)* Notice there are two things we are to do, both using the word "not" - *"Fear thou not;"* and *"be not dismayed"*. On the other hand there are seven phrases describing what God does for us. Twice He says "I am," three times "I will" and twice "yea", reminding us that we can surely count on God. In summary we have two things for us not to do, and seven things God does. That is good reason to rejoice, knowing, that God is on our side.

In order to capture and cast down the enemy thoughts that don't comply with the eight guidelines, we need to ask God to help us resist the temptation to meditate upon the wrong thought and move directly to our thought replacement plan.

As we read through the Psalms of David we will notice this is the tactic he employs every time he describes his fears, terrors, loneliness and the feeling of being overwhelmed. He rapidly changes thought gears as the Holy Spirit moves him to pen words that recalibrate his thinking back towards the character and works of God. His writings move from a moment of crisis to confession, and on to a celebration of the goodness of God. The following Psalm is an example of this pattern and describes a point in his life when he was overwhelmed yet his thoughts turned to God and praise.

"Hear my cry, O God; attend unto my prayer. From the end of the earth will I cry unto thee, when my heart is overwhelmed: lead me to the rock that is higher than I. For thou hast been a shelter for me, and a strong tower from the enemy. I will abide in thy tabernacle for ever:

I will trust in the covert of thy wings. Selah. For thou, O God, hast heard my vows: thou hast given me the heritage of those that fear thy name. Thou wilt prolong the king's life: and his years as many generations. He shall abide before God for ever: O prepare mercy and truth, which may preserve him. So will I sing praise unto thy name for ever, that I may daily perform my vows." (Psalm 61:1-8).

Another of David's psalms that show a similar thought pattern is his song of deliverance written during a time of anguish and betrayal whilst fleeing from his son Absalom. Watch how David's shift in thinking lifts him up from his anxiousness.

"LORD, how are they increased that trouble me! many are they that rise up against me. Many there be which say of my soul, There is no help for him in God. Selah. But thou, O LORD, art a shield for me; my glory, and the lifter up of mine head. I cried unto the LORD with my voice, and he heard me out of his holy hill. Selah." (Psalm 3:1-4).

Think on these things!

Chapter 7

THE PROBLEM WITH "I"

I AM ABASED

Faith and Humility are a solution to Anxiety

In 1898, from March to December, two male African lions, known locally as "The Ghost" and "The Darkness", killed a number of construction workers on the Kenya-Uganda Railway. The attacks took place at the Tsavo River in Kenya and halted the project until they were hunted down and shot by a British foreman, Lieutenant-Colonel John Henry Patterson. The incident was described in a book titled "The Man-Eaters of Tsavo" that in 1996 became the basis for a movie starring Michael Douglas and Val Kilmer. The significance of this pair of man-eating lions was their unusual behaviour and attacks. Over the nine months the two lions stalked the campsite, dragging Indian workers from their tents at night and devouring them. Crews tried to scare off the lions and built campfires and thorn filled fences around their camp for protection, but to no avail; the lions leaped over or crawled through the thorn fences. Patterson set traps and tried several times to ambush the lions at night from a tree. After repeated unsuccessful attempts, he shot the first lion on 9 December 1898. Patterson writes in his account that he wounded the first lion with one bullet from a high-calibre rifle. This shot struck the lion in its back leg, but it escaped. Later, it returned at night and began stalking Patterson as he tried to hunt it. He shot it through the shoulder, penetrating its heart with a more powerful rifle and found it lying dead the next morning not far from his platform. Twenty days later, the second lion was found and killed. Patterson claimed it died gnawing on a fallen tree branch, still trying to reach him. The first lion killed measured 2.95 metres (9 feet 8 inches) from nose to tip of tail. It took eight men to carry the carcass back to camp. Patterson kept the skulls from both lions, and used their skins as rugs. In 1924, he sold the remains of the man-eaters to the Field Museum in Chicago, where they were mounted and put on display in 1928. They are still there today.[19]

There is a lion lurking for you

We can all imagine the fear those two lions put into Patterson and the workers whilst the big cats were roaming around seeking whom they may devour. We must likewise always be aware that someone is hunting us. The lion lurks quietly in tall grass, stalking our every step, waiting for a moment to catch us off guard. If we stray from the group, put down our weapons, or doze in the sun, our enemy will strike. It is this strategy of fear the apostle Peter wrote about when warning of Satan's mode of offence, *"Be sober, be vigilant; because your adversary the devil, as a roaring lion, walketh about, seeking whom he may devour:" (1 Peter 5:8).*

As I mentioned in the introduction of this book, one of Satan's

---

19 https://www.dailykos.com/stories/2014/4/9/1250842/

greatest desires is to cause us to become fearful and potentially thrown into a state of anxiety, just as though we are like the frightened workers wondering when the next attack is coming from the lion lurking in the darkness.

What God wants us to know in these moments is that as Christians we have a heavenly Father who loves us and values us more than anything else in the world. He totally cares for us. Our cares may be many and varied, but God has only one care - us! We can cast anything and everything on Him because of His desire to care for us. Hence in the verse preceding the mention of the devil as a roaring lion, Peter encourages us to release our anxieties to God, *"Casting all your care upon him; for he careth for you."* (1 *Peter 5:7)*.

There is a real enemy on the prowl after you

Satan knows our weaknesses and our strengths. He's had thousands of years to observe humankind and has become an expert on human nature. In fact, Satan knows the depths of our depravity far better than we do. We must never forget that we are his prey and that this roaring lion is ravenous with hunger. He prowls and pounces when we least expect it, which explains our need to remain alert and sober. He loves to keep us locked up and bound in fear of his imminent attack on our hearts and minds.

Whoever lives under the impression that Satan doesn't exist is living in a fantasy world. After witnessing my wife live with and manage a mental illness, including panic attacks, for nearly a quarter of a century, I certainly believe in the reality of Satan and his principalities and powers. Satan goes by several names in the Bible. The term *diabolos*, "devil," is used. This title refers to his slander of God's people." The Greek word *Satanas*, "Satan," comes from a Hebrew word for "adversary." In Revelation 9:11, he is called *Abbadon* and *Apollyon*, meaning "Destroyer," names that refer to his destructiveness. Together these and other labels for our enemy describe him as a dangerous, destructive deceiver who slanders and accuses us at every opportunity. The book of Revelation describes his future and final fall from the heavens, *"And the great* **dragon** *was cast out, that old* **serpent***, called the* **Devil***, and* **Satan***, which* **deceiveth** *the whole world: he was cast out into the earth, and his angels were cast out with him. And I heard a loud voice saying in heaven, Now is come salvation, and strength, and the kingdom of our God, and the power of his Christ: for the* **accuser** *of our brethren is cast down, which* **accused them** *before our God* **day and night***."* (Revelation 12:9-10).

Because our *"adversary the devil"* is on the prowl like a lion hunting for prey, we must be *"sober"* and *"vigilant"* ever alert to his attacks against our heart and mind. Whilst we must respect his power, there is no reason to overestimate his power. We respect him, like an electrician respects the power of electricity but we are not to fear him or revere him. Too many Christians do this. They believe that anything bad that happens to them comes directly from the devil or his demons. But this is as much a mistake as underestimating his power. Satan isn't the immediate cause of all suffering and sin. As sinful human beings we can all do enough damage to ourselves and others without the devil's involvement. Furthermore, the world system offers its own enticements and allurements that can take a vicious toll on the quest of a Christian to live right before God.

However, there is no need to be overcome by Satan and to let him confuse our mind until it is entirely taken up with meditating on our worries, anxieties, and fears. As Christians our mind is under the blood of Jesus Christ, and we are sealed by the Holy

Spirit. We've been purchased with a price, which is the precious blood of Christ, and our whole being - mind, body, and soul - is under the blood. Just like those mentioned in Revelation, we too have access to the efficacy of the work of Christ in our lives, *"And they overcame him by the blood of the Lamb, and by the word of their testimony; and they loved not their lives unto the death."* *(Revelation 12:11).*

Run or Resist?

The response of the Christian to the attack of the devil is not what most people would do. Using the analogy of a roaring lion coming towards us, the natural response would be to turn and run in panic, yet Peter gives us a faith response and implores us to RESIST! - *"Be sober, be vigilant; because your adversary **the devil**, as a **roaring lion**, walketh about, seeking whom he may devour: Whom **resist** stedfast in the **faith**, knowing that the same afflictions are accomplished in your brethren that are in the world."* *(1 Peter 5:8-9).*

The word "resist" means to "stand against, oppose." But this command is met with a vital qualification. We don't resist Satan with confidence in our own power or ability. Any time we do that, we're overmatched. We are to *"resist stedfast in the faith"*. In other words, be firm and grounded in what we believe and stand with unshakeable faith in our all-powerful God, relying on His defence to stand against the evil lies and works of the devil. - *"Wherefore take unto you the whole armour of God, that ye may be able to **withstand** in the evil day, and having done all, to **stand**."* *(Ephesians 6:13).*

James, the half-brother of Jesus, was inspired by the Holy Spirit to pen his epistle in which he affirms to us the need to stand confidently against Satan on the basis of our submission to the almighty God: "*Submit yourselves therefore to God. Resist the devil, and he will flee from you.*" *(James 4:7).* Both Peter and James knew that believers can win a decisive victory over Satan when we realise that we have insufficient strength in and of ourselves. But when we turn to our Lord and draw on His limitless power through faith, we can stand against the adversary.

This brings us to the topic of humility and submission before God as a weapon we must use to overcome anxiety.

The power of Humility to overcome anxiety

Let's come back to the roaring lion in 1 Peter. Within the scriptural context of the call to resist the attacks of the devil, Peter laid out some clear principles on humility as a precursor to overcoming anxiety and thereby being able to resist the devils roar.

When you read 1 Peter 5:5-7 you will notice that verse 7 concerning casting our care upon God is not a *command* but the *result* of putting into practice the call to humility in verses 5 and 6. If you look carefully at the text you will notice the precise punctuation. There is no full stop at the end of verse 6 but rather a colon indicating verse 7 is a continuation of thought from the preceding verse. I have placed the verse numbers here to allow you to see what I am referring to, "*5 Likewise, ye younger, submit yourselves unto the elder. Yea, all of you be subject one to another, and be clothed with humility: for God resisteth the proud, and giveth grace to the humble. 6 Humble yourselves therefore under the mighty hand of God, that he may exalt you in due time: 7 Casting all your care upon him; for he careth for you.*" *(1 Peter 5:5-7).*

Sometimes we quote verse 7 as a stand-alone command without realising it is the result of the outworking of verses 5 and 6 in our lives.

Are you wearing Humility today?

The passage begins with a metaphor which pictures a servant putting on an apron before serving those in the house. Perhaps Peter is recalling that last supper in the upper room where Jesus girded Himself with a towel and washed the disciples' feet (John 13:4-17). We are to *"be clothed with humility."* Humility is when you are free from pride and arrogance. You know that in your flesh you are inadequate, yet you also know who you are in Christ. In a sense we 'wear' humility, it is seen in our attitude and actions. We are to put it on and tuck it in. We are to wear it around the house, at work, at church, and in the community. It is not an easy garment to put on, but it is most becoming. When we think about an example of this we must agree nobody ever wore the clothing of humility quite like Jesus. – *"Let this mind be in you, which was also in Christ Jesus: Who, being in the form of God, thought it not robbery to be equal with God: But made himself of no reputation, and took upon him the form of a servant, and was made in the likeness of men: And being found in fashion as a man, **he humbled himself**, and became obedient unto death, even the death of the cross." (Philippians 2:5-8).* Jesus wore humility as though it were a royal robe to grace the shoulders of a king. We too, are to be clothed with humility and the best place to put on that garment is Calvary as we deny ourselves and die to self each day and put His desires first and foremost. *"Then said Jesus unto his disciples, If any man will come after me, let him **deny himself**, and take up his cross, and follow me." (Matthew 16:24).*

The upper Hand

In the Bible, God's hand symbolizes both His discipline in correcting belief and behaviour as in this verse in the Psalms, *"For day and night **thy hand** was heavy upon me: my moisture is turned into the drought of summer. Selah." (Psalm 32:4)*. It also represents deliverance by God and his protection as seen in His rescue of the Israelites from Egypt, *"I prayed therefore unto the LORD, and said, O Lord GOD, destroy not thy people and thine inheritance, which thou hast redeemed through thy greatness, which thou hast brought forth out of Egypt with **a mighty hand." (Deuteronomy 9:26)*.

When we humble ourselves *"under the mighty hand of God,"* we willingly accept His discipline as being for our good and for His glory. We gratefully acknowledge His deliverance and protection that is always in His time and in His way. This is why we must humble ourselves before God at all times. It is the means by which we gain God's grace rather than His hand of resistance. This is how we gain the upper hand in the war with anxiety.

The problem is in the "I"

This is a powerful truth to grasp and to realise submission and humility are keys to defeating anxiety rooted in pride. How can a person suffering from anxiety also have pride? How is being proud connected to being full of care? It is not that we feel proud about the anxiety. On the contrary many people feel embarrassed, stigmatised and ashamed. But we feel proud about what is causing the anxiety.

For example, a stressed anxious person may say things like, "I have to be the one who handles the future, I am the one who takes care of the kids, I have to be the one who fixes the outcomes of our ageing parents." They will say "It's okay, this is **my** lot in life, it's what I have to bear, it's **mine** to handle – **I've** got this." But "this" is causing anxiety through worry and fear.

In pride we carry around all of our uncertainties, insecurities, unknowns, and we think "I have to carry this, it's mine, I can do this, and **I've** got this."

You will notice the middle letter in the words "pride" and "anxiety" is the letter "I". We have an "I" problem that is the root of fear and creates the anxiety.

There is clearly a connection between having freedom from anxiety and with possessing humility. Humility is the door to liberation from care.

The root of anxiety is pride because pride is telling us that I can control the outcome of my life. Humility recognises that God controls everything. The answer to anxiety is to humble ourselves and say "I'm not in charge of my pregnancy"; "I'm not in charge of my child"; "I'm not in charge of my finances". When we worry, we have a lack of confidence in our ability to control a situation. Humility says, "God you are in charge and I am under your MIGHTY hand!"

If you listen to everything that you are telling yourself and therefore create anxious thoughts in your heart – it is because you have "I" at the centre of your conversations, thoughts and life. You say things like "What will I do now?" "How will I deal with ..." etc. Instead you need to humble yourself and place God in the centre of your life and trust that God's mighty hand is strong enough to protect you from the lion's temptations as he attacks you with fear and panic.

When we humble ourselves we are acknowledging that God is in control and we will trust, follow, lean upon and hold on to

His hand. Otherwise it's the reverse – we are trusting, following, leaning upon and holding onto ourselves.

Humility knows "I can't do this by myself." Humility says, "I am aware of the fact that I can't control things, my kids, my future, my job or the economy. I need God every moment."

Anxiety stems from carrying something we weren't meant to carry. Maybe that thing we're anxious about is not ours to carry or control. This is why when we humble ourselves under the mighty hand of God the *result* of this decision has a casting effect. Our cares are cast from us to the Lord Who has the ability and strength to sustain us. *"Cast thy burden upon the LORD, and he shall sustain thee: he shall never suffer the righteous to be moved." (Psalm 55:22).*

Casting your care is the Result not a command

1 Peter 5:7 is a not a command. It is the result of humility. As we humble ourselves, we actually are casting our care and ridding ourselves of anxiety. We don't hold on to our care any longer – We are careful for nothing and our care no longer holds onto us because we are now emotionally, mentally and spiritually relying on God completely and holding on to His mighty hand.

When we try to get rid of anxiety and ask God to take it away without humbling ourselves, God says, 'I am not going to take the anxiety away until you put away the pride that carries it.'

The apostle Peter had learnt on numerous occasions that trying to do things his own way pridefully never worked out well.

Cast it on the Right side

Consider the word *"casting."* You can picture the disciples casting their garments on the donkey for Jesus to sit upon, *"And they brought the colt to Jesus, and **cast** their garments on him; and he sat upon him." (Mark 11:7).* Perhaps when Peter penned this word he was remembering what his brother and he were doing when Jesus called them to follow him, *"Now as he walked by the Sea of Galilee, he saw Simon* (also known as Peter) *and Andrew his brother **casting** a net into the sea: for they were fishers." (Mark 1:16).* When those anxieties begin to weigh you down, we cast them like a cloth or net from our grip.

One night after fishing all night and catching nothing, Jesus tells Peter to cast his net on the right side of the ship and he would make a catch. Previously in Peter's life he had resisted the fishing suggestion of Jesus until he reluctantly did what Jesus asked. In that instance, after catching a miraculous haul of fish, Peter fell on his knees in humility before his Lord and said *"Depart from me; for I am a sinful man, O Lord." (Luke 5:8).* This time when Jesus suggested they cast on the right side after toiling all night and catching nothing, Peter humbled himself and cast the net. *"**Cast** the net on the right side of the ship, and ye shall find. They **cast** therefore, and now they were not able to draw it for the multitude of fishes." (John 21:6).* Notice the pattern; humility resulted in casting, which led to success.

With this pattern in mind, let's review the verses with some specific words highlighted, *"Likewise, ye younger, **submit** yourselves unto the elder. Yea, all of you be **subject** one to another, and be clothed with **humility**: for God resisteth the **proud**, and giveth **grace** to the **humble**. **Humble yourselves** therefore under the **mighty hand** of God, that he may **exalt you** in due time: **Casting** all your **care** upon him; for he **careth** for you. Be sober, be vigilant; because your adversary the devil, as a **roaring lion**, walketh about, seeking whom he may devour: Whom **resist** stedfast in the faith, knowing* *that the same afflictions are accomplished in your brethren that are in the world." (1 Peter 5:5-9).*

The matter is Settled

Peter concludes his discussion on anxiety and gives his testimony of what happens when we apply Biblical principles when panic attacks. He says in effect, "I know about the lion's roar. I know about pride and trying to cast it my way. I know about the loss of focus and seeing the waves. I know about the panic and thinking God doesn't care. "I" was at the centre of my thinking, feeling and actions, but when I humbled myself under the mighty hand of God, He stepped in and exalted me in His due time. Then He settled me and the panic attack was gone!"

Though victory is certain, Peter reminds us that suffering and pain will accompany the battle. No one who has endured an enemy attack emerges without some measure of pain. The battle will shake us, shock us, and often leave ugly scars in our hearts, minds and, sometimes in our bodies. But when the dust settles Peter lists the benefits that come with God's heavenly version of the "Purple Heart", *"But the God of all grace, who hath called us unto his eternal glory by Christ Jesus, after that ye have suffered a while, make you **perfect, stablish, strengthen, settle** you. To him be glory and dominion for ever and ever. Amen." (1 Peter 5:10-11).*

The God who is bigger than anxiety has a special interest in you, **He careth for you.**

Chapter 8

CASTING TECHNIQUES

I CAN APPLY

Applying your Faith to overcome Anxiety

My wife Jenny and two of my sons, Ben and Joshua, love to fish. They tell me there is a special knack to casting a line effectively. Whether it is casting bait or a lure, using a fishing line out over the water, or whether it's throwing a cast net in the shallows; it takes some skill and various learned techniques. Depending on the type of fishing involved, the casting style can vary from the finesse of using a flick of the wrist, to a two-handed method to gain added distance to reach inshore fish, utilising the entire body in the cast. Whatever the casting method it seems everyone adds his own secret personal touch. If you are really dedicated and specialised in casting you may even compete in Casting as a sport which is supervised by the International Casting Sport Federation and has members in 31 countries. It is included in the World Games and has been considered for the Olympics. Casting can be a serious business!

Thankfully, when it comes to casting our care upon the Lord, the spiritual methods are the same for everyone and available to all, and not just those who have a 'knack' for casting. As I mentioned in the previous chapter God welcomes those burdened with anxiety to cast their cares upon Him by following the admonition, *"Humble yourselves therefore under the mighty hand of God, that he may exalt you in due time: Casting all your care upon him; for he careth for you." (1 Peter 5:6-7).*

Whilst the very act of humbling ourselves before God and handing the control over to Him has the effect of casting our care upon Him, there are also many other Biblical and practical methods anxiety sufferers can employ to reduce, release and remove the anxiety from their body, heart and mind. We must also remember God exalts us and lifts us up in due time - His timing, not ours. It's rare that anxiety disorders will disappear in an instant. It is generally a period of time of healing and recovery. We must continue to trust the process of healing as we cast our care upon Him.

Before we examine the various Biblical casting practices I need to briefly mention a common medical profession casting method.

Cognitive Behavioural Therapy (CBT)

In the medical and psychology fields there is a variety of helpful psychological therapies that are used for the treatment of anxiety disorders. The strongest evidence of effectiveness is Cognitive Behavioural Therapy. This treats panic attacks by changing our thoughts (cognition) towards anxiety, and the way we react (behaviour) to anxiety or panic attack triggers. Once the patterns of thinking and acting that are adversely affecting our anxiety are recognised, then we can make changes to replace our patterns with new ones that reduce anxiety and improve coping.

CBT starts with helping people to understand why they have anxiety attacks, in hopes of reducing the symptoms and identifying the triggers of their attacks.

I am not a medical doctor and cannot comment on the clinical effectiveness or otherwise of CBT, other than from what I have read about the treatment. Personally, I have witnessed some positive results from my wife's few experiences with CBT.

However, as a Christian and a pastor I would like to also recommend an additional form of CBT. For the purpose of this book, I have called it TBC (**T**hinking **B**iblically about **C**are) based on the principles of casting your cares upon the Lord as a means to help you scripturally and practically apply your faith in God in overcoming anxiety and panic attacks.

In keeping with the casting concept, I have taken the liberty to label each of the techniques as a type of casting method to help you keep in mind the idea of giving the care to God. This list is by no means exhaustive and is simply a collection of casting techniques that have been effectively utilised in my pastoral ministry and with Jenny.

The Salvation Cast

The first step to an anxiety-free mind is to give our life to Jesus Christ and to ask Him to be our Lord and Saviour. In 1965 Evangelist Billy Graham wrote, *"Historians will probably call our era 'the age of anxiety.' Anxiety is the natural result when our hopes are centred in anything short of God and His will for us. At its best, anxiety distracts us from our relationship with God and the truth that He is 'Lord of heaven and earth.' At its worst, anxiety is a crippling disease, taking over our minds and plunging our thoughts into darkness. But God wants so much more for us than to walk through life full of fear, worry and anxiety."* [20]

God no longer wants us to live in unbelief. He wants us to believe that He is able, by His Spirit to overcome this torment.

The Lord desires every person to have a personal relationship with Him. We must believe that Jesus Christ came to earth as God in the flesh, lived a perfect life, and then voluntarily died on a cross, because He loves us. On that cross, He literally paid for all of our sins. He took our blame! He punished Himself for our wrong-doings. What a great gift! John 3:16 says *"For God so loved the world, that he gave his only begotten Son, that whosoever believeth in him should not perish, but have everlasting life."* God, in His awesome love, came to earth to make a way for us to be forgiven of our sins and given eternal life.

Finally, we must place our full trust in Jesus Christ as our personal Saviour. Romans 10:13 says, *"For whosoever shall call upon the name of the Lord shall be saved."* In verse ten of that same chapter God says, *"For with the heart man believeth unto righteousness; and with the mouth confession is made unto salvation."* He says it's as simple as believing and receiving. It's as simple as asking.

On a personal note: if you've never asked Jesus Christ to be your personal Saviour, you could do that right now! With Him in your heart, life will make a lot more sense. You could stop right now and sincerely pray something like this:

Dear Lord Jesus, I am a sinner. I believe that you died for my sins and rose again for me. Please forgive all my sin, come into my heart, and take me to Heaven when I die. I now accept Your gift of eternal life. Thank you for saving me. Amen.

As a Christian you will have the help of the Holy Spirit to guide you, lead you, teach you and comfort you as you read the Bible, pray and seek to live according to Biblical principles. Humility is

---

20 https://billygraham.org/story/how-to-overcome-fear-anxiety-and-worry/

choosing to live God's way when before salvation we were living for ourselves.

The Thought Replacement Cast

There are many voices in this world, all competing for our attention. We need to tune into the voice of God and allow His words to permeate our thoughts. Keep listening to God more than having anxious thoughts and feelings. We can do this as we meditate on the Word of God, listening to uplifting worship music or reading "faith" filled material. As we continue choosing to redirect our attention away from anxiety and toward trusting God, our anxiety will continue decreasing, and peace will increase.

Taken collectively, our anxious thoughts are like a monster that is created by the way in which we perceive what happens in your life. What voice we believe determines what we perceive. We can either choose to believe the voice of God through His Word and Holy Spirit, or we can believe the voice of fear speaking to our heart and mind. Remember, anxiety is rooted in fear and as we look ahead into the future and project our fear, we hear the roar of the lion and a panic attack ensues. It is in these moments we need to have a thought replacement chart to refer to.

I suggest you review the eight guidelines to think upon, that I wrote about in Chapter 6, and write down a personal list to correspond with each word from Philippians 4:8. For example:

Write down some things that are **true** from God's Word about Who you are in Christ, and meditate on these. Recognise the lies of Satan and replace them with the truth from God. Ask God to help you view your life from the correct perspective so you can recognize what's real versus what's false and what's true versus what's untrue.

Write down a list of things that are **honest, just, and pure** and then ponder on these things and thank God for them. Keep in mind that you're not powerless against your fears. Even if the worst of your worries were to come true, there is much you can do to deal with them in the power that God offers you. He promises to walk through every inch and second of it with you. His Holy Spirit is your comforter. Jesus said, *"And I will pray the Father, and he shall give you another Comforter, that he may abide with you for ever;" (John 14:16)*.

Concentrate on people and Bible promises that are **lovely** and of a **good report**. In times of anxiety you should avoid social media and other forms of media that will feed your fears with negativity and terror. Instead, find some Christian friends and talk with them face to face ensuring that your thinking is according to God and His Word. Remember WWJT.

Reflect only on things of **virtue** which have moral goodness and holiness. Avoid thinking of matters that rob you of wholeness.

Finally, spend some time recording things you can **praise** God for. Remember to count your blessings and name them one by one.

The Prayer Cast

One of the best ways to rid ourselves of anxiety is by replacing our worry and tension with prayer and thanksgiving. Anxiety hits us from all directions. Whether it be school stress, work stress, a stressful family situation, or anything else in life that causes us to feel unsettled, tired, and afraid of the future; anxiety can feel like it's taking over our lives. This is why we must heed the admonition of the apostle Paul to turn our care into prayer from Philippians 4:6-7.

We must turn to the One who is in control of all things. God holds all of our lives in his hands and is the only one who can calm our minds when we experience the inner storm and have created the 'wind and the waves within.' The only way to gain peace in the midst of anxiety is to turn to God, trusting in His perfect will and His power to hold us in His hands. The Bible is loaded with promises from God to call upon Him in prayer and He will hear our voice, *"And call upon me in the day of trouble: I will deliver thee, and thou shalt glorify me." (Psalm 50:15).*

In his book, "Walking through the Darkness," Neil Anderson suggests the following prayer for those troubled by fear:

"Dear Heavenly Father, You are the fortress, shield and strength of my life. I refuse to be intimidated by any fear object. I choose to sanctify Christ as the Lord of my life. You are the only omnipotent, omnipresent God. You have not given me a spirit of fear. By Your presence in my life I have power, love and a sound mind. Your power enables me to live a responsible life. Your presence in my life has made me a partaker of Your divine nature so I can love others as You love them. You are my sanctuary, and I ask You to protect my family... Amen."[21]

The Simplify Cast

A common source of anxiety is feeling that we are stretched too thinly between many commitments that are seemingly competing for our time. These could be commitments to our family, church, work, school, sport, and hobbies etc. One way to cast your care is by asking God for wisdom and discernment for times we need to say "No".

Jesus knew time pressures can create stress and anxiety and

---

21 https://billygraham.org/answer/

said to his overworked and tired disciples, "...*Come ye yourselves apart into a desert place, and rest a while: for there were many coming and going, and they had no leisure so much as to eat.*" *(Mark 6:31).* We must give ourselves permission to relax at times.

Generally if we are stressed because of time constraints we are living at a velocity that deep down we know is unsustainable, and this in itself is creating anxiety. Life is too crammed with busyness and we keep waiting for things to get better, but they never do. We need to simplify, declutter and give ourselves some breathing room and margin. When life is cluttered with too many activities, the stress of trying to keep up with it all can fuel anxiety.

Planning ahead also makes a difference. When we plan ahead for major events or projects and take time to prepare, this can help cut back the anxiety.

To practically utilise the simplify cast, we need to examine our schedule and consider what we can cut out to eliminate unnecessary stress and anxiety. Pray for the wisdom we need to identify specific changes to make, so that our activities truly reflect our priorities. Avoid living in the tyranny of the urgent. Instead, prioritise to focus on accomplishing the important things. This in turn reflects the values that God wants us to have.

The Questioning Cast

Anxiety can become a problem when our body tells us that there is danger when there is no real danger. This can be triggered by overestimating and/or catastrophizing. When you overestimate, you believe something that highly unlikely is about to happen; for example, when we believe that we will faint or die as a result of a panic attack. Catastrophizing is when we imagine the worst possible thing is about to happen and that we will not be able to cope. For example: "I'll embarrass myself and everyone will laugh" or "I'll freak out and no one will help." This type of thinking is often related to social concerns such as embarrassing oneself.

In both of these situations you need to question the past to help reveal the unrealistic nature of your thoughts. The apostle Paul calls this type of thinking 'strongholds' that need to be cast down. They seem real and true but they are vain imaginations. We must remember not every thought or emotion we have is necessarily true. We must question the validity of the thought and practice, *"Casting down **imaginations**, and every high thing that exalteth itself against the knowledge of God, and bringing into captivity every thought to the obedience of Christ;" (2 Corinthians 10:5).* For example, here are some questions to ask yourself:

- What am I afraid will happen? *When I'm having a panic attack, I am afraid that I won't be able to breathe or that I'll die.*
- How many times have I had this thought when I am having a panic attack? *A lot!*
- How many times has it actually happened? *Never. Even when it feels like I am going to die, nothing bad has happened. However, what if THIS is the time it happens?*
- How many times have I had that thought? *Many times.*
- How many times has it actually happened? *Never.*
- How likely is it that it will really happen? *The chances of something bad happening are extremely small.*

It's important to remind yourself of that when you are having a panic attack. You may need to have this prewritten somewhere so that you can fix your mind on it through the process of the attack.

The Bible Verse Cast

The greatest source of truth is the Word of God. *"Thy word is true from the beginning: and every one of thy righteous judgments endureth for ever."* *(Psalm 119:160)*. As we learn to take God at His Word and work it out in our lives, our fears will melt away and be replaced by peace from God. We need to fill our mind with the positive truths of Scripture by reading the Bible often, studying it, memorizing, and applying it. When we make your own personal list of the Scripture promises that focus on our identity as God's child we can regularly read them aloud and claim them as our personal belief. Here is a list of a few precious words from God concerning each one of us:

* All things are possible with Christ - *"I can do all things through Christ which strengtheneth me."* *(Philippians 4:13)*.
* God can give me the grace I need - *"And God is able to make all grace abound toward you; that ye, always having all sufficiency in all things, may abound to every good work:"* *(2 Corinthians 9:8)*.
* I am accepted by God - *"To the praise of the glory of his grace, wherein he hath made us accepted in the beloved."* *(Ephesians 1:6)*.
* I can be satisfied with God - *"Blessed are they which do hunger and thirst after righteousness: for they shall be filled."* *(Matthew 5:6)*.
* I am in Jesus and will remain in Him - *"But the anointing which ye have received of him abideth in you, and ye need not that any man teach you: but as the same anointing teacheth you of all things, and is truth, and is no lie, and even as it hath taught you, ye shall abide in him."* *(1 John 2:27)*.

- I am a child of the heavenly Father - *"And if children, then heirs; heirs of God, and joint-heirs with Christ; if so be that we suffer with him, that we may be also glorified together." (Romans 8:17).*

- I belong to God - *"But ye are a chosen generation, a royal priesthood, an holy nation, a peculiar people; that ye should shew forth the praises of him who hath called you out of darkness into his marvellous light:"(1 Peter 2:9).*

- I am blessed with every spiritual blessing - *"Blessed be the God and Father of our Lord Jesus Christ, who hath blessed us with all spiritual blessings in heavenly places in Christ:" (Ephesians 1:3).*

- I am a friend of God - *"Ye are my friends, if ye do whatsoever I command you." (John 15:14).*

- I am precious in God's sight - *"Since thou wast precious in my sight, thou hast been honourable, and I have loved thee: therefore will I give men for thee, and people for thy life." (Isaiah 43:4).*

- I have power, love, and a sound mind - *"For God hath not given us the spirit of fear; but of power, and of love, and of a sound mind." (2 Timothy 1:7).*

- God will never forsake me - *"Let your conversation be without covetousness; and be content with such things as ye have: for he hath said, I will never leave thee, nor forsake thee." (Hebrews 13:5).*

- I have victory through Jesus - *"But thanks be to God, which giveth us the victory through our Lord Jesus Christ." (1 Corinthians 15:57).*

The Holy Spirit is our guide, teacher and comforter and He uses the Bible to reveal the Father's will and purposes for our life. Therefore our daily prayer should be the same as the Psalmist, *"Search me, O God, and know my heart: try me, and know my thoughts: And see if there be any wicked way in me, and lead me in the way everlasting." (Ps 139:23-24).* The Holy Spirit will personally comfort you and teach you how to live according to God's Word.

The Confession of unbelief Cast

It is important to realise we may be harbouring a sin of unbelief and need to confess it unto God and receive His forgiveness for our heart attitude. The writer of the book of Hebrews warned, *"Take heed, brethren, lest there be in any of you an **evil heart of unbelief**, in departing from the living God." (Hebrews 3:12).* Anxiety is one of the evil conditions of the heart that comes from unbelief. Jesus has said that anxiety comes from doubt, worry and little faith. The root of a sinful condition of the heart is unbelief in the living, Almighty God.

We need to take time to confess each of our worries in prayer to God and ask Him to forgive us for not trusting in His care; then stop for a moment and think how many different sinful actions and attitudes come from anxiety. Anxiety about finances can give rise to coveting, greed, hoarding and stealing. Anxiety about succeeding at some task can make us be irritable and abrupt towards others. Anxiety about relationships can make us be withdrawn and indifferent with other people, especially with those we love. Anxiety about how someone will respond to us can make us cover over the truth and lie about things.

We battle unbelief by meditating on God's word and asking for the help of his Holy Spirit as we seek to internalise the promises of God and apply them to our lives. For example when I become anxious about decisions I have to make about the future, I battle unbelief with the promise: *"I will instruct thee and teach thee in the way which thou shalt go: I will guide thee with mine eye." (Psalm 32:8).* Another example is when I am anxious about facing a difficult person or situation, I battle unbelief with the promise: *"What shall we then say to these things? If God be for us, who can be against us?" (Romans 8:31).*

The Rejoicing today Cast

Anxiety will dredge up stressful memories from the past or make us worry about what may happen in the future. But God wants us to live in the present and rejoice in the day He has given us. *"This is the day which the LORD hath made; we will rejoice and be glad in it." (Psalm 118:24).* Don't allow fear of tomorrow to rob us of our blessings and joys of today. We need to simply trust in God to help us live every day that He gives us for the best. Often times praising God is hard when our thinking is anxious and our emotions are feeling negative. It is in these moments we offer up our praise as a sacrifice to God, *"By him therefore let us offer the sacrifice of praise to God continually, that is, the fruit of our lips giving thanks to his name." (Hebrews 13:15).*

The Breathing Cast

Like a lion lunging out from tall grass, so too out of the blue, without warning, can come that overwhelming sense of dread and fear that grips us. Our heart pounds so loudly that our ears ring and the sudden onset of panic leaves us frozen with anxiety. When the Old Testament prophet described a similar startling event in his life, he said it took his breath away, *"For how can the servant of this my lord talk with this my lord? for as for me, straightway there remained no strength in me, **neither is there breath left in me.**" (Daniel 10:17).*

A physical technique to help reduce that racing anxious feeling is to practice calm breathing. Be still. Find a quiet space and focus on breathing. Just inhale slowly and deeply through the nose, pause, and then exhale through your mouth. This is a strategy that we can use to help reduce some of the physical symptoms experienced during a panic attack. We tend to breathe faster when we are anxious, which can make us feel dizzy and lightheaded. This in turn can make us even more anxious. During an episode of anxiety we start to hyperventilate (or take in rapid breaths cutting off the carbon dioxide levels in your blood and causing light-headedness). Calm breathing helps our nervous system to relax.

The Healthy practices Cast

Anxiety not only affects the mind and heart but also our body. As we are a whole being, all our parts are connected. Though anxiety may start in the mind, it can trigger very real physical symptoms like headaches, chest pain, an increased heart rate, dizziness, and numbness in the arms, hands and fingers. Often, physical symptoms can heighten the anxiety, making us worry more.

Our bodies are the temple of the Holy Ghost and the vehicles God uses to work through. We must use them for His glory: "*What? know ye not that **your body is the temple of the Holy Ghost** which is in you, which ye have of God, and ye are not your own? For ye are bought with a price: therefore **glorify God in your body**, and in your spirit, which are God's.*" *(1 Corinthians 6:19-20).*

If we are suffering from anxiety we need to consider our body and health, because poor health habits can exacerbate anxiety without our even realizing it. We must make sure to get sufficient sleep and undertake some physical exercise, maintain a healthy diet (that includes fruits, vegetables, whole grains, lean proteins, limited sugar, and eliminate caffeine), and drink plenty of water.

There is a high correlation between those who don't exercise and those who experience anxiety.[22] Even though in writing to Timothy, the apostle Paul said, *"bodily exercise profiteth little:" (1 Timothy 4:8)*, it still does profit something! Exercise can be a way of calming a racing mind. The endorphins released during physical exercise will often help flood the body and mind with feelings of calm and happiness. If we are not in a routine of regular exercise we may want to start with gentle exercises such as walking, biking or swimming.

While these factors may not be the sole reasons we experience anxiety, neglecting to keep a healthy balance in these areas can be more harmful than we realize. Developing these habits can improve our peace of mind, knowing that we are doing the best we can to make wise, responsible decisions in this area of our health.

The Medicine Cast

We live in a world where people take medication for just about everything. This is especially common for those with anxiety, because anxiety often causes physical symptoms that encourage people to see a doctor. In severe cases of anxiety, doctors may prescribe medications (i.e., anti-depressants or mild tranquilizers). These are an attempt to soothe and calm a person down to help alleviate the onset of a panic attack. From my limited knowledge of these types of medications, I believe they are designed to work quickly to slow down brain activity and the over-stimulation of the nervous system when a panic attack occurs.

If you are wondering if you should or shouldn't take medication

---

22 https://www.ncbi.nlm.nih.gov/pmc/articles/PMC3632802/

for anxiety, I can tell you that God knows all about your situation, and He loves you and wants to help you overcome it. This can happen as you learn to cast your cares into His hands. This doesn't mean it's necessarily wrong for you to be on medicine for anxiety; it may be one of the ways God uses to help you. Our minds and our bodies are enormously complex; sometimes things don't work the way they should, and medicine may be helpful. We must also remember what may work for one person may not work for another.

However, whilst medication can help relieve the physical symptoms, thus decreasing the fear associated with them, lowering your stress level alleviates anxiety. If you learn how to overcome anxiety through casting your cares upon God, you should be able to successfully manage or cure your anxiety without any chemical help.

If you are already taking medication, do not cease without first seeking medical advice.

The Avoiding triggers Cast

Dealing with unpleasant people or situations can also trigger anxiety. If someone consistently seems to cause you to feel anxious, consider talking with him or her about it. If that person will not change any behaviour, consider reducing the amount of time you spend with him or her. This may be easier said than done in some circumstances where you can't avoid a situation that produces anxiety. However, you may be able to alter the situation so that it doesn't cause as much anxiety. Often, this means taking a new approach to it, or trying out new communication tactics.

For example, if your daily commute to work makes you feel anxious because you're afraid of crashing your car because you are feeling anxious or nervous, then consider taking public transport or catching a ride with someone else. You probably can't avoid going to work, but you can alter how you get there to reduce your stress. At least until you're at a point where you can handle driving again. This doesn't have to be forever!

Perhaps you're feeling anxious because your friend keeps calling you every day to "check-up" on you. You can try telling her how you feel: "I appreciate that you want to make sure I'm doing okay, but having to give you daily status reports is making me feel like I'm under a lot of pressure, and I'm feeling pretty stressed. What if you call me just on the weekend instead? I can catch you up on everything I'm doing then."

The Godly Counsel Cast

The Bible tells us the wise person seeks counsel and knows it is a place of safety: "Where no counsel is, the people fall: but in the multitude of counsellers there is safety." (Proverbs 11:14). Sadly, there is a stigma in our culture that seeking help through counselling or therapy means you are weak or lack faith. However, this could not be further from the truth. Remember, countless people suffer from anxiety each day, and only a small fraction seek help. You are not alone! If your anxieties continue or increase, I strongly suggest that you see a competent Christian Biblical counsellor or professional for additional help.

The Worship Cast

When we are struggling with worry, sadness and anxiety, there is a sure fire treatment that God prescribes, it is "the garment of praise *for the spirit of heaviness;" (Isaiah 61:3).* God has not designed us to walk in a state of anxiety, depression, or hopelessness but in joy, praise, and victory. As we read the Psalms we will notice David singing his songs of praise to overcome his cares and worries. The songs of David refocused his mind and heart from his troubles, stresses and cares to the only One who can relieve Him of his stress – God: *"Why art thou cast down, O my soul? and why art thou disquieted in me? hope thou in God: for I shall yet praise him for the help of his countenance." (Psalm 42:5).*

When experiencing anxiety, choose to audibly declare, praise and thank Him for the things He has done. Praise Him in advance for the things which you are still awaiting a spiritual breakthrough. Select some God-affirming and honouring songs to add to your playlist and listen to them to lift your spirits. Join in with the weekly worship service at church and lift up your voice in song as you prepare to hear His Word spoken in the service. Don't neglect the house of worship in your anxious times, it is then when you may need the people of God the most.

As we offer our worship to the Lord it reminds us that Jesus is greater than whatever we face in our lives.

The Songs in the night Cast

It seems the worst time for my wife, Jenny, when she had panic attacks was at night. Possibly in the stillness and darkness our thoughts are amplified in our minds. In his distress, Job said, *"Terrors take hold on him as waters, a tempest stealeth him away in the **night**." (Job 27:20).* During stressful times David pens his thoughts and feelings during the night watches: *"I cried with my whole heart; hear me, O LORD: I will keep thy statutes. I cried unto thee; save me, and I shall keep thy testimonies. I prevented the* *dawning of the morning, and cried: I hoped in thy word. Mine eyes prevent the **night watches**, that I might meditate in thy word. Hear my voice according unto thy lovingkindness: O LORD, quicken me according to thy judgment. (Psalm 119:145-149).*

This is why we need to ask God for songs in the night. The anxious Psalmist wrote, *"I call to remembrance my **song in the night**: I commune with mine own heart: and my spirit made diligent search." (Psalm 77:6).* Again Job found his solace through the messages from God in song through the night seasons, *"But none saith, Where is God my maker, who giveth **songs in the night**;" (Job 35:10).*

If you feel you need to see a doctor by all means go and see a doctor, but don't discount that praise can start to lead you out of the darkness. There is something very freeing, soothing and reassuring to know God is with you in the dark nights of the soul and praising Him in those moments: *"Yet the LORD will command his lovingkindness in the daytime, **and in the night his song shall be with me**, and my prayer unto the God of my life." (Psalm 42:8).* When we praise and worship in our struggle it lifts our gaze up and off whatever is bringing the darkness, and puts our focus back on Jesus. After all, He says, *"Thou art my hiding place; thou shalt preserve me from trouble; thou shalt compass me about with **songs of deliverance**. Selah." (Psalm 32:7).*

The song "No Longer Slaves" by Bethel beautifully describes this thought.

You unravel me with a melody, You surround me with a song
Of deliverance from my enemies 'til all my fears are gone
I'm no longer a slave to fear, I am a child of God [23]

---

23 https://www.azlyrics.com/lyrics/bethelmusic/nolongerslaves.html

The Patience Cast

Nobody who suffers from anxiety enjoys the experience. Each person I have spoken to desires to be rid of the affliction instantly. Whilst nothing is impossible for God and He can heal you immediately if He chooses to do so, it is often a process of time before you come out of the darkness.

However, God uses this healing time to cause us to draw closer to Him and become totally dependent on His care as we wait patiently upon His timing: *"Rest in the LORD, and wait patiently for him: fret not thyself because of him who prospereth in his way, because of the man who bringeth wicked devices to pass." (Psalm 37:7).* God does hear your cries and is the expert therapist and counsellor who will lift you up in due time as you follow His Biblical principles and commands.

David encourages us as God inspired him to pen these words *"I waited patiently for the LORD; and he inclined unto me, and heard my cry. He brought me up also out of an horrible pit, out of the miry clay, and set my feet upon a rock, and established my goings. And he hath put a new song in my mouth, even praise unto our God: many shall see it, and fear, and shall trust in the LORD." (Psalm 40:1-3).*

If you pause and realise just how much an anxious life costs you; physically, mentally, spiritually and emotionally, it should help you wait patiently and give you the resolve to keep on going and not quit during the casting process. Jesus advised us to always count the cost of our choices, actions and decisions. In a parable describing what it is like to be a disciple and devoted follower of Christ, He said, *"For which of you, intending to build a tower, sitteth not down first, and **counteth the cost**, whether he have sufficient to finish it? Lest haply, after he hath laid the foundation, and is not able to finish it, all that behold it begin to mock him, Saying, This man* *began to build, and was not able to finish." (Luke 14:28-30).* Remember that overcoming anxiety is something that takes serious commitment. Most people want to stop panic attacks and anxiety overnight and that is understandable, but you must trust the process and allow God to work. Peter lets us know we may very well suffer a while through the anxiety before it's all over, but it's worth it in the end if we keep casting our care upon the Lord and trusting in Him. Peter who knew first-hand what it was like to be taken and sifted by Satan said, *"But the God of all grace, who hath called us unto his eternal glory by Christ Jesus, **after that ye have suffered a while**, make you perfect, stablish, strengthen, settle you."* *(1 Peter 5:10).*

The Lion of the tribe of Judah is on my side

You can rest assured that whatever you face God is greater than all your fears, *"The LORD is my light and my salvation; whom shall I fear? the LORD is the strength of my life; of whom shall I be afraid?"* *(Psalm 27:1).*

God's truth is speaking strong and sure to the deepest core of our soul – *"Fear not!"*

Replace those fearful thoughts with His words of truth and sleep in peace tonight, *"I laid me down and slept; I awaked; for the LORD sustained me." (Psalm 3:5).*

He knows what concerns you, He's got you covered, *"Behold, he that keepeth Israel shall neither slumber nor sleep." (Psalm 121:4).*

Hold onto the promise that the devil's roar will one day be silenced by the roar of the lion of the tribe of Judah – Jesus!

ABOUT THE AUTHOR

After completing a law degree and pursuing a career in law, God called Robert Bakss to the ministry in 1988. Pastor Bakss, who accepted Jesus Christ as his personal Lord and Saviour in 1979, often states God called him from "man's law to God's law"! He is currently the Senior Pastor of Lighthouse Baptist Church, Rockhampton, Queensland, Australia and has been there since 1997. Over the past few years the Lord has established his ministry and blessed the church in a wonderful way for the glory of God. His influence throughout churches in Australia, the South Pacific and parts of Asia has increased as he has helped many pastors and missionaries through his preaching, teaching and the annual Pastors Refresher School. His vision of training preachers, missionaries and Christian workers for the twenty-first century was realized with the founding of Australian Baptist College in 2007. Dr. Bakss is also the author of *Worship Wars - What the Bibles says about Worship Music* and *Poles Apart - A Christian couple gives bipolar a voice*. He and his wife Jenny have five children, three of whom are now married, they have been blessed with nine grandchildren.

You can connect with Dr. Bakss through:
Email: info@robertbakss.com
www.robertbakss.com
Facebook.com/robert.bakss
Twitter.com/RobertBakss

CPSIA information can be obtained
at www.ICGtesting.com
Printed in the USA
FSOW03n1459010218
44059FS